TEACHING VOCABULARY

50 CREATIVE STRATEGIES, GRADES 6–12

Second Edition

Gail E. Tompkins
California State University, Fresno, Emerita

Cathy Blanchfield
Duncan Polytechnical High School, Fresno

PEARSON

Merrill
Prentice Hall

Upper Saddle River, New Jersey
Columbus, Ohio

Library of Congress Cataloging in Publication Data

Teaching vocabulary: 50 creative strategies, grades 6-12/[edited by] Gail E. Tompkins, Cathy L. Blanchfield. — 2nd ed.
   p. cm.
   Includes bibliographical references.
   ISBN-13: 978-0-13-240503-4 (alk. paper)
   ISBN-10: 0-13-240503-2
   1. Vocabulary—Study and teaching (Secondary)—United States. 2. Language arts (Secondary)—United States. I. Tompkins,
   Gail E. II. Blanchfield, Cathy L.
   LB1631.T337 2008
   372.61—dc21   2007015958

Vice President and Executive Publisher: Jeffery W. Johnston
Senior Editor: Linda Ashe Bishop
Senior Development Editor: Hope Madden
Senior Production Editor: Mary M. Irvin
Senior Editorial Assistant: Laura Weaver
Design Coordinator: Diane C. Lorenzo
Cover Designer: Candace Rowley
Cover Image: Images.com
Production Manager: Pamela D. Bennett
Director of Marketing: David Gesell
Marketing Manager: Darcy Betts Prybella
Marketing Coordinator: Brain Mounts

This book was set in Novarese by Carlisle Communications, Ltd. It was printed and bound by Courier Kendallville, Inc. The cover was printed by Phoenix Color Corp.

Pearson Education Ltd.   Pearson Education Australia Pty. Limited
Pearson Education Singapore Pte. Ltd.   Pearson Education North Asia Ltd.
Pearson Education Canada, Ltd.   Pearson Educación de Mexico, S.A. de C.V.
Pearson Education—Japan   Pearson Education Malaysia Pte. Ltd.

10 9 8 7 6 5 4 3 2 1
ISBN-13: 978-0-13-240503-4
ISBN-10:   0-13-240503-2

PREFACE

Teaching Vocabulary: 50 Creative Strategies, Grades 6–12 grew out of an informal focus group among teacher-consultants in the San Joaquin Valley Writing Project in Fresno, California. We met throughout the year to discuss standards implementation and our experience with middle and high school students' literacy needs. One concern in particular resurfaced again and again: We realized we must better meet the needs of students who come to us with limited vocabulary development, particularly English learners who are an integral and large part of many of our classrooms.

A lack of vocabulary development affects students' reading comprehension and their writing skills. This can be particularly damaging as students move through middle and secondary grades, when content area reading requires so much vocabulary learning, influencing future success and career choices. Vocabulary learning particularly affects the success of English learners; but when vocabulary instruction is done well, it can help close the gap in reading and writing performance for all students.

Once the need was defined, we set about finding the solution. We read articles and books about vocabulary development, experimented with teaching techniques in our classrooms, and shared stories of our successes. Each of the 50 lessons in this compilation grew out of this experience, practice, and exploration of meaningful vocabulary instruction. Each author has taken special care to discuss the steps in preparing and teaching the strategy, to explain where the strategy fits into the overall curriculum, and to describe how their students responded. Every strategy is appropriate for middle and secondary students, grades 6–12.

TEXT ORGANIZATION

We have organized ideas into six sections:

1. Collecting and Sorting Words
2. Exploring Definitions
3. Working with Meanings
4. Expanding Writing Vocabulary
5. Investigating Word Origins
6. Playing with Words

When students learn vocabulary words, understanding develops over time. The more experiences they have with a word, the deeper their understanding. The first two sections (Collecting and Sorting Words, Exploring Definitions) contain activities that promote a first or second experience with a word. The third and fourth sections (Working with Meanings, Expanding Writing Vocabulary) contain activities that enable students to understand words at a deeper level. Students are encouraged to use the words in multiple contexts. Once they gain this deeper understanding, students can use the words to expand their vocabularies by adding affixes and finding new ways to use the words through play (Investigating Word Origins, Playing with Words).

The San Joaquin Valley Writing Project is part of the National Writing Project (NWP), and there are NWP sites in every state. If you are interested in learning more about the NWP or in joining your local site, contact the National Writing Project through its website at *http://www.writingproject.org* or call (510) 642-0963.

ACKNOWLEDGMENTS

In addition to the many students whose responses to these strategies helped us to shape and refine them, we are indebted to the reviewers of our manuscript for their suggestions, comments, and insights: Rebecca F. Brown, Wake Forest University; Jackie Glasgow, Ohio University; Joseph W. Guenther, University of Wisconsin, Platteville; James Johnston, Central Connecticut State University; Margot Kinberg, National University; and Susan N. Wood, Florida State University.

CONTENTS

WORKING WITH MEANINGS   61

EXPANDING WRITING VOCABULARY   91

Note: Every effort has been made to provide accurate and current Internet information in this book. However, the Internet and information posted on it are constantly changing, so it is inevitable that some of the Internet addresses listed in this textbook will change.

"ROBUST" VOCABULARY INSTRUCTION

Kathleen Godfrey

Robust. This is a word often associated with a healthy individual. Yet when experienced readers encounter the phrase "robust vocabulary instruction" (Beck, McKeown, & Kucan, 2000), they easily switch to another meaning of the word; in this phrase, *robust* means solid, multidimensional, extended, well-thought-out vocabulary instruction. Good readers are able to understand differences in meaning based on the context in which a word is used. However, many middle school and high school students have difficulty understanding vocabulary and differentiating among meanings of words. These students, whose vocabularies have limitations due to youth and inexperience, encounter words in classrooms that are unfamiliar and difficult. Teachers may be able to read assigned texts easily, but their students find the same texts difficult or even incomprehensible.

Research suggests that vocabulary and reading comprehension have a strong link in readers' ability to understand what they read increases as they learn new words (Lehr, Osborn, & Hiebert, 2004). Margaret McKeown and Isabel Beck (2004) propose two ways that teachers can increase student vocabulary: 1) through class conversations employing new words; calling attention to ways vocabulary words can be utilized, focusing on student vocabulary choices, allowing for word play, and otherwise promoting word consciousness; and 2) through direct instruction. Teachers need to create classrooms in which students pay attention to words, their applications, and the word choices writers, teachers, and the students themselves make. Moreover, one or two usages of the word are not enough; teachers must repeat words, embedding them in instruction/classroom discussion, in order to increase the likelihood of student mastery. One study suggests that students must encounter a word 6 to 10 times before that word becomes part of their reading vocabulary (Marzano, 2004). Clearly, teachers must create multiple ways in which students experience targeted vocabulary.

In addition, learners benefit greatly from direct vocabulary instruction. Robert Marzano (2004) analyzes a number of studies, concluding that direct vocabulary instruction is beneficial in expanding background knowledge and enabling students to understand disciplinary knowledge. However, teachers should keep in mind that not all vocabulary instruction is equally effective. In essence, they need to understand the underlying principles that create a strong vocabulary component in the classroom. Rather than moving students through a vocabulary workbook or arbitrarily selecting 10 words each week that students are quizzed on, teachers need to create research-based vocabulary instruction that advances student mastery of words and meanings.

IMPORTANT ELEMENTS OF "ROBUST" VOCABULARY INSTRUCTION

But what principles should inform teachers' choices about vocabulary instruction? A survey of recent work on vocabulary instruction suggests a number of elements that should be part of vocabulary instruction.

Students Must Learn How to Use Context Clues to Uncover Meaning, but They Must Also Understand That This Technique Does Not Always Work

Readers increase their vocabulary through frequent, active reading. One way to help students' vocabularies grow is through teaching about context clues. Readers can use synonyms, definitions, or other contextual information to understand a word. However, McKeown and Beck (2004) argue that not all word meanings can be discovered through context. They explain that contexts can be classified in ways that reflect their relationship to individual word meanings: directive, general, nondirective, and misdirective. The first category, directive, is the only one that helps students derive meaning in a relatively precise way. General contexts provide ways for students to discern a general meaning. Nondirective contexts do not provide help in discovering meaning, and misdirective contexts actually steer readers to identify a meaning that does not correspond to the actual meaning of the word. When reading a text together, teachers can call attention to the ways that context and individual word meanings interact.

Students Must Be Actively Involved in Learning Vocabulary

Since context clues are not always helpful, teachers also need to use direct instruction so students become actively engaged in learning words and their meanings. Passive practices, such as copying dictionary definitions and memorizing them, are not effective. In fact, Robert Marzano (2004) summarizes one study that concluded students who did not understand a word were still able to come up with a serviceable definition if they understood the structure of dictionary definitions. Students must be actively involved in thinking about meaning, describing meaning in their own words, and using the word in new settings. Moreover, students should be introduced to academic language, specifically the vocabulary associated with academic pursuits and disciplinary knowledge. Highlighting these vocabulary words and encouraging students to be actively engaged in understanding and using academic language ultimately allows students to become independent learners.

Students Must Understand Concepts in Order to Understand Related Words

Lehr, Osborn, and Hiebert (2004) suggest that students will have greater success remembering a word if it is linked to a concept with which they are already familiar. Words that "provide precision and specificity" (p. 22) become part of students' web of factual and conceptual knowledge surrounding a particular concept. Thus, teachers need to both select words linked to familiar concepts and enrich students' experience of words/concepts through sensory and experiential means as well as through repetition (Feathers, 1993).

Students Must Understand That There Are Levels of Knowing a Word

Researchers divide the levels of understanding a word into three categories: *association, comprehension,* and *generation* (Baker, Simmons, & Kame'enui, 1995). The first level of word knowledge is association. Students first understand the word in a specific context or based on the definition. The understanding is simple, introductory, and bound by context. Awareness of a word moves to the comprehension level when one can classify, identify definitions, and find synonyms and antonyms. This level of understanding can accommodate new situations of usage, but there is still room for growth. The last level of comprehension, generation, occurs when one is able to "generate" meaning—that is, create personal, individualized understanding or application of a word. Teachers need to help students move toward generative understandings of words, and students who are aware of their level of comprehension can push themselves to work toward applying the words in different contexts.

Students Must Learn About Dictionaries and Morphology

Dictionary definitions adhere to conventions of writing. For example, definitions of nouns begin with a classification of the word, followed by what distinguishes the word from its class (e.g., a *cup* is a container with a handle). Definitions of verbs and adjectives often contain synonyms and/or descriptions. If students understand that a number of definitions actually contain a derivative of the word itself, they can then refer to the original word. Understanding these conventions can help students master the ability to use dictionaries successfully.

Proficient readers use morphology to uncover the meaning of unfamiliar words. As Edwards, Font, Baumann, and Boland (2004) explain, students will be better equipped to understand words if they are able to 1) divide words into prefixes, suffixes, and root words (e.g., *unpredictable* = *un-* + *predict* + *-able*); 2) understand each part of a word (e.g., *un-* = not; *predict* = to foresee; *-able* = able to do so); and 3) recombine these parts to create meaning (e.g., *unpredictable* = not able to foresee something).

Classroom Practices Should Include Opportunities for Nonlinguistic Representations of Meaning

Research shows that students' understanding of new words is more long-lasting when they experience the words both linguistically and nonlinguistically. Marzano (2004a) explains that memory is stored in both linguistic and nonlinguistic modes, thus emphasizing the importance of both types of experience for learning. Creating mental images, drawing pictures, or acting out a word can help make meaning more concrete and connected with what students already know. Thus, incorporating nonlinguistic activities in vocabulary instruction is vital to full comprehension of a word.

Classrooms Should Promote Language Awareness and Play

Creating classrooms in which student awareness of word choice is heightened means helping students focus on the importance of precision in vocabulary, but also on the ways writers play with language for various purposes and effects. Johnson, Johnson, and Schlichting (2004) define a number of categories of word play including the study of expressions, word associations, and word manipulations. Activities may include games like creating literal representations of idioms or highlighting the "sparkly" or especially evocative words that authors use. Playing with words promotes a deeper understanding of meaning and/or a greater consciousness of how words work.

Vocabulary Study Should Include Attention to Cognates, Especially for English Learners

For students whose primary language is Latin-based, studying cognates can be one method of increasing vocabulary. Nash (1997) estimates that 10,000–15,000 words are Spanish-English cognates. Lehr et al. (2004) approximate that between one-third to one-half of the words used on a regular basis by educated English speakers are cognates. Spanish speakers who understand that *vender* means "to sell" and that the English words *vendor* and *vend* share the Latin root of *vender* (*venus*, meaning "sale") will be able to approximate meaning. Mastery of cognates can quickly increase English learners' vocabulary.

Teachers who understand these principles create classrooms characterized by robust vocabulary instruction. Moreover, teachers who understand research behind word selection can make pedagogical choices that ensure classroom vocabulary instruction will promote student success.

WORD SELECTION

At the foundation of vocabulary curriculum should be an understanding of how to best select words on which to focus. Choosing words to highlight is crucial to student mastery. For the purposes of vocabulary instruction, theorists have organized words into three tiers. Tier One consists of words that students generally know and use in their everyday lives such as *child*, *school*, and *table*. Tier Three encompasses words that students will rarely encounter—often words that are specific to content knowledge like *isthmus* or *synecdoche*. Research suggests that rather than focusing on Tier One or Tier Three words, students are better served by attention to Tier Two words, that is, words that experienced language users will encounter in more sophisticated and complex settings. Beck, McKeown, and Kucan (2000) give examples of Tier Two words: "*coincidence, absurd, industrious*" (p. 16). These theorists also explain criteria teachers can use in identifying appropriate Tier Two words to target for direct instruction. Teachers should identify words in upcoming reading assignments that are typically understood by experienced readers. They should consider their students' ability to articulate the concepts associated with new words. Direct vocabulary instruction should focus on words that will give students more precise and varied ways of expressing familiar concepts. Among the words identified, teachers should then consider which ones best communicate the meaning of the passage and/or which can be used in a number of ways in class in order to help students develop a complex understanding of the associated concept.

TEACHING IDEAS FOR 6–12 CLASSROOMS

Students need to understand why vocabulary instruction is necessary and how they can use newly learned words to improve reading comprehension. This book provides a variety of activities middle and high school teachers can use to develop and extend students' vocabulary. Teacher consultants from the San Joaquin Valley Writing Project at California State University, Fresno, have collaborated on this text. Each lesson grows out of experience, practice, and exploration of meaningful vocabulary instruction. We have organized teaching ideas into six sections:

- Section One: Collecting Words
- Section Two: Exploring Definitions

- Section Three: Working with Meanings
- Section Four: Expanding Writing Vocabulary
- Section Five: Investigating Word Origins
- Section Six: Playing with Words

Although this text presents classroom practices informed by research and theory, the lessons themselves must be embedded in classroom practices that encourage student awareness of their cognitive strategies, inspire discovery, and promote appreciation for language. The teachers who created these lessons offer them as models and as contributions to well-designed, research-based, robust vocabulary instruction.

REFERENCES

Baker, S., Simmons, D., & Kame'enui, E. (1995). *Vocabulary acquisition: Synthesis of research.* Eugene, OR: National Center to Improve the Tools of Educators.

Beck, I. L., McKeown, M. G., & Kucan, L. (2000). *Bringing words to life: Robust vocabulary instruction.* Bethesda, MD: National Reading Panel.

Edwards, E. C., Font G., Baumann, J. F., & Boland, E. (2004). Unlocking word meanings: Strategies and guidelines for teaching morphemic and contextual analysis.
In J. F. Baumann & E. J. Kame'enui (Eds.), *Vocabulary Instruction: Research to practice* (pp. 159–178). New York: Guilford.

Feathers, K. (1993). *Infotext: Reading and learning.* Scarborough, OH: Pippin.

Graves, M. F., & Watts-Taffe, S. M. (2002). The place of word consciousness in a research-based program. In A. E. Fastrup & S. J. Samuels, *What research has to say about reading instruction* (3rd ed., pp. 140–165). Newark, DE: International Reading Association.

Johnson D. D., Johnson B. V. H., & Schlichting, K. (2004). Logology: Word and language play.
In J. F. Baumann & E. J. Kame'enui (Eds.), *Vocabulary instruction: Research to practice* (pp. 179–200). New York: Guilford.

Lehr, F., Osborn, J., & Hiebert, E. H. (2004). *A focus on vocabulary.* Honolulu, HI: Pacific Resources for Education and Learning.

Marzano, R. J. (2004). *Building background knowledge for academic achievement: Research on what works in schools.* Alexandria, VA: Association for Supervision and Curriculum Development.

McKeown, M. G., & Beck I. L. (2004). Direct and rich vocabulary instruction. In J. F. Baumann & E. J. Kame'enui, *Vocabulary instruction: Research to practice* (pp. 13–27). New York: Guilford.

Nash, R. (1997). *NTC's dictionary of Spanish cognates: Thematically organized.* Lincolnwood, IL: NTC Publishing Group.

"You Will Thank Me for This Some Day": A Reflection on Direct Vocabulary Instruction

Faith Nitschke

For the past several years, direct vocabulary instruction has been on my teaching menu. I recognize that the best way to increase one's vocabulary is through wide reading, but unfortunately, very few of even our "best" students read widely for enjoyment. As a result, students, especially those planning to attend college, complain that their vocabulary is limited and express a desire to expand their knowledge of words. Direct vocabulary instruction seems a reasonable way to increase our students' vocabulary.

A few years ago, I conducted an informal study on direct vocabulary instruction with my sophomore Gifted and Talented Education (GATE) class and used their insights to shape my future instructional practice. At the end of that year, I asked students for a metacognitive response to direct vocabulary instruction (written anonymously) about their experiences in my class. I use the word *metacognition* frequently with my students; we regularly examine many of my practices and units—especially when I try something new. In my purposeful naïveté, I imply that all learners should be metacognitive thinkers: people who think about their thinking. Much of the information presented here is a result of their responses.

BACKGROUND

During the year of this informal research, we had four vocabulary "units." The first unit contained words from our core novel, *Lord of the Flies* (Golding, 1954). In their reading journals, students were to write down three words from each chapter that were new or unknown to them. When we were about three-fourths of the way through the book, I had the students look back through their words and choose one they felt was challenging and "important." Students "announced" the word they wanted to teach (to avoid any overlapping of words) by listing them in alphabetical order on the chalkboard. For this unit, the students taught the words using Vocabulary Squares, a lesson found in this book. The second vocabulary unit consisted of Greek and Latin root words taken from an SAT preparation manual. For these, students were required to make flashcards as well as demonstrate the word's versatility in English by making posters, showing all the words that can be formed from the root. The third unit consisted of words the students randomly selected but felt were important. These might be words that they had heard, read, or wanted to learn; words from a word-a-day pad on my desk; or words chosen from a dictionary. The students were to teach their word by singing it, acting it, dancing it, or otherwise making it memorable—activities described in Golub's *Activities for an Interactive Classroom* (1994). The last unit consisted of words from another core novel, *To Kill a Mockingbird* (Lee, 1960). Students were allowed to teach their word using any method they chose. Many made a poster of their word, often just with the definition and perhaps a sentence. Some marginally prepared students wrote just the word and its definition on the board. Students were also required to write a test question for their word to be used on the test.

In the following sections, I share some of the results found in my students' metacognitive responses. These results and comments have shaped my direct vocabulary instructional practice and, I believe, have made my vocabulary teaching efforts more effective than they had been in the past.

TEACHING STRATEGIES

One practice that the students strongly recommended is having the students teach their words rather than having a teacher just assign words for students to study independently. Students felt that posters were not very valuable as a teaching aid, and that they best remembered words that were delivered the most memorably. Students the previous year were still talking about Vanessa's teaching of the word *vehement*, where she was so loud and forceful during her presentation that the teacher next door came into the room to see if everything was okay! The students felt that the presentation should be worth more than a few points (more than just a homework grade, more like a quiz grade) to "push" students past the mere poster stage. They felt anyone who just made a poster should get a C. Different methods of teaching words were used, but the students felt the interactive methods were superior to more sedate deliveries; teachers know, of course, that variation in methodology is important to provide a stimulating classroom. Fortunately, the focus of this book is to present many successful vocabulary teaching strategies that will appeal to the various learning styles of students.

SELECTION OF WORDS

So, where do we get suitable words for teaching? Content-area teachers are in an ideal position to isolate key words from the text for direct instruction because these words are often crucial to the student's comprehension of the related concept. Think of the many words necessary to teach a unit on photosynthesis, for example. This crucial reliance on student comprehension of key words does not usually occur in literature—except perhaps for a few key words, often unique to the setting. Therefore, restricting vocabulary choices only to core texts is not as necessary as in content classes where students must comprehend the meaning of key words that together work to explain a concept. Sometimes, in fact, restricting new vocabulary words only to those found in the currently studied piece of literature that does not contain a particularly rich vocabulary can result in ludicrous situations. For instance, my daughter one year was required to learn the words *baobab*, *yar*, and *aft*, all taken from one of the stories in her fifth-grade anthology. In my 50+ years, I have never had the opportunity (or the desire) to use the word *baobab*. Challenging core novels, however, often require students to "stretch," and hence provide an opportunity for students to encounter frequently used, sophisticated words—ideal words for vocabulary study. One caveat here: Teachers do need to monitor the words to be taught to avoid archaic, technical, or inappropriate choices.

In support of using literary texts for vocabulary words is the following incident: My eleventh-grade student aide was typing a vocabulary test composed of the questions written by my sophomores. He expressed his amazement to me that he recognized many of the words from *Lord of the Flies* in the novel he was reading in his junior English classroom and how much typing the sophomores' questions had helped him understand vocabulary he was encountering in other books.

Therefore, in a language arts classroom, ultimately it does not really matter where the words come from, as long as they are rich, challenging words that educated people encounter in their wide reading experiences. And sometimes there are unexpected bonuses from this: For instance, Gilbert that year had randomly chosen a word out of the dictionary to teach. When we were taking the state-mandated standardized test, he literally jumped up out of his chair. "Oh, my gosh!" he exclaimed. "My word is on the test!" As the students left the room, many of them thanked Gilbert.

TESTING STRATEGIES

Students also wrote a test question about their word that would be on the test—which is an excellent strategy for a variety of academic (and selfish) reasons. The students also stated that they should be tested on the words. Yes, they actually desired the "push" of a test to force them to learn the meanings of the words. (Isn't metacognition wonderful?) Not only that, they said they needed to be tested more than once on the same words because of the brain research on retention I had shared with them previously; so to honor their requests, vocabulary tests became cumulative so that subsequent tests also contained words studied from previous units.

REINFORCEMENT OF STUDIED WORDS

One suggestion made by the students is that they should be encouraged (and rewarded) for actually using new words. I began to circle vocabulary words embedded in essays and jotted a note of praise. When students used new vocabulary words orally in class, we "oohed" and "a ahed." Another strategy is to require the students to use the words in a piece of writing; this can even be a paragraph or two.

An important factor in acquiring new words is usage. Students need to know the part of speech of the word being taught, and how it changes (inflects) in its different sentence functions. There are many ways to accomplish this. One possibility I have used: When a student taught a word, the other students were required to use the word in a sentence on a strip of paper (I cut used photocopies into fourths and students wrote on the clean side). The student/teacher collected and corrected these and handed them back. I spot-checked these and used any discrepancies as a "teachable moment." This put the focus on learning on the students.

Serious, college-bound students recognize their limited vocabularies and are anxious to increase their word banks; hence, they participate cheerfully (well, . . . almost). But, many of our students may not immediately appreciate this need for direct vocabulary instruction, but it's sort of like our parents said to us, "You will thank me for this some day."

REFERENCES

Golding, W. (1954). *Lord of the flies*. New York: Putnam.

Golub, J. N. (1994). *Activities for an interactive classroom*. Urbana, IL: National Council of Teachers of English.

Lee, H. (1960). *To kill a mockingbird*. Philadelphia: Lippincott.

Collecting Words

1. Personal Word Walls
2. Thematic Word Walls
3. Vocabulary Building: Sometimes Less Is More
4. Animal, Vegetable, or Mineral
5. Disastrous Words
6. Vocabulary Carousel: A Merry-Go-Round of Words
7. Sorting for Success
8. Vocabulary Squares
9. Parts-of-Speech Word Wall

Researchers acknowledge that students need multiple exposures to a word before they understand it while reading and can use it in their own speaking and writing (Marzano, 2004). When students are first introduced to words, the learning process begins. Even though this first contact with words must be followed with other activities, teachers want it to be meaningful for students by encouraging them to be actively involved in the initial contact with the word. Beck, McKeown, and Kucan (2002) explain that just copying a definition does little for students' comprehension of a word. Collecting words enables students to learn words at what Baker, Simmons, and Kame'euni (1995) call the *associative level*, or the level at which students understand only one meaning of a word, with little or no understanding of its nuances or connotations. This is the beginning level of understanding, a necessary level for further building.

This first chapter is a set of activities that enable students to begin the process of learning a word. To some secondary teachers word walls and other collections are for elementary school, but these activities are quite effective with older students. According to Allen (1999) "word walls are absolutely essential in our classrooms" (p. 70). Long after the vocabulary activity is over, learning continues because the wall remains in view. Faith Nitschke, Kathleen Markovich, Eileen Boland, and

Jared Kaiser have written articles explaining four very different ways of collecting and arranging words for word walls in their classrooms.

Martha Dudley and Carol Surabian use word walls, but ask students to sort the words on the wall. Sorting words is another strategy that has been often used in the elementary classroom and is now adapted to secondary classrooms. According to Bear, Invernizzi, Templeton, and Johnston (2004), "word sorting offers the best of both constructivist learning and teacher-directed instruction" (p. 61). They continue by explaining how students can enhance their vocabularies by sorting activities. Tamara Harritt, Laurie Goodman, and Cynthia Stovall describe classroom-proven examples about how this is the case with secondary students.

REFERENCES

Allen, J. (1999). *Words, words, words: Teaching vocabulary in grades 4–12.* York, ME: Stenhouse.

Baker, S., Simmons, D., & Kame'euni, E. (1995). *Vocabulary acquisition: Synthesis of research.* Eugene, OR: National Center to Improve the Tools of Educators.

Bear, D. R. Invernizzi, M. Templeton, S., & Johnston, F. (2004). *Words their way: Word study for phonics, vocabulary, and spelling instruction* (3rd ed.). Upper Saddle River, NJ: Merrill/ Prentice Hall.

Beck I. L., McKeown, M. G., & Kucan, L. (2002). *Bring words to life: Robust vocabulary instruction.* New York: Guilford Press.

Marzano, R. (2004). *Building background knowledge for academic achievement: Research on what works in schools.* Alexandria, VA: Association for Supervision and Curriculum Development.

PERSONAL WORD WALLS

1

Eileen Boland

The pencil taps lightly on the surface of the dark brown desktop. A sheet of paper rests next to the ever-moving pencil. The Giver, a novel by Lois Lowry (1991), lays open to page 98. Concentration is etched across Mai's face. Her eyes follow the endless trail of words.

"I think I'll add release to my chart. This word is important because it tells what happens to people in the community when they get old," she says to herself in a slight whisper.

"Memory is another important word because Jonas is receiving memories from the Giver." Her pencil glides to the letter M on the chart making a gentle scratching sound as she adds the word.

"Hmm, I wonder what the next words will be from this chapter I'm going to read. I'm really starting to collect a lot of good words." The pencil rests now as Mai picks up the book and enters the world of Jonas and the Giver once again

What is Mai doing? This student is collecting and categorizing self-selected words on a personal word wall chart as she reads T*he Giver* (see Figure 1–1). She is placing them alphabetically by the first letter of the word.

Mai selects these words for a number of reasons. Primarily, these words are significant to the story; they move the plot along and reveal the inner workings of life in the community. Mai also knows these words will help in her reading and writing. She will most likely encounter these words again and again in the story, so she can focus on the meaning of the passage. In writing, her personal word chart will serve as a quick reference tool for responding in literature logs, creating open-mind portraits, and designing character sketches. The teacher may construct word sorts based on student lists. The uses for the chart are numerous.

During grand conversations, Mai can refer to her word wall chart as a spark for ideas to share with the class. Also, it can be used as a supplemental word source for the class word wall. During this time, Mai can share some of the words from her list. By the same token, as other students share their words, she can add them to her personal collection.

By gathering words, Mai is integrating the words into her repertoire of language. Most importantly, Mai and her classmates are deepening their understanding of the story they are reading. The construction of meaning is at the heart of this strategy.

FIGURE 1–1 A student's
Personal Word Wall

A	B C	D	E F	G
anguished assignments	community counsel		emotional escape	Giver

H	I J	K L	M	N
	Jonas	Lily	memories	nurturer

O	P Q	R	S	T
obedient overwhelm	pain	regret release	successor	transgression training

U	V	W X	Y	Z

THE STORY LINE

As we begin our literature study, a class word wall is put on display. It is composed of a large sheet of butcher paper that is divided up according to the alphabet. The students add important words to this chart that coincide with the word collecting on their personal word wall charts. The steps in using this strategy are:

1. Pass out personal word wall chart.
2. Direct students to select important words that help them understand what they are reading.
3. Read the first chapter and model for the students how to select key words.
4. Guide students as they choose words from the first chapter.
5. Read Chapter 2 and have the students select words to add to their charts.
6. Discuss possible choices and add these to the class word wall.
7. Continue this process as students read the novel.
8. Select five of the most important words at the end of the novel and write about their significance to the story. Their importance must be exemplified by using specific examples from the novel.

During the reading of *The Giver*, I reinforce students' use of these words through oral or written activities. I emphasize the words on the word wall in journal writing, word sorts, open-mind activities, grand conversations, word posters, word webs, and character sketches.

CONCLUSION

The lifeless pencil rises again. Twisting slowly between the thumb and the forefinger, the pencil anticipates its breath of life. Then, in a moment, it stops. The lead is in place under T. In a fluid motion, the word *transgression* is spelled out. "This word is so important. It means. . . ." These words fade into the hollows of her throat as Mai analyzes the purpose of this word. She is just beginning her journey into new worlds of language, using her personal word wall chart.

REFERENCE

Lowry, L. (1991). *The giver*. Boston: Houghton Mifflin.

2

THEMATIC WORD WALLS

Jared J. Kaiser

Walking into my classroom the first day of school, students immediately notice words hanging on the classroom wall. I hear a new student to the school grumble, "He's gonna make us write."

A 20-foot banner of butcher paper hangs horizontally on the wall; a memento from last year's class. It is covered with file cards, and a word is written on each file card.

One student sits quietly, pondering the banner and suddenly exclaims, "Oh! I see. It says FRIENDS." Excitedly she asks, "Do we get to make one of those?"

Another new student adds, "I like drawing. Do we get to draw pictures, too?"

Several other students begin showing interest in this wall of words, mostly commenting on the pictures and the artists' abilities.

Regardless of the specific conversations, my students are starting the year in a very productive way. They are talking about words, and looking at the use of words differently. For me, this is the most appropriate place to begin the writing process.

The thematic word wall has a number of advantages. My classroom instruction is centered on a theme each quarter; all content curriculum is loosely tied to this theme. The first day of the theme is always exciting as the students file in to read our new theme on the word wall. I have prepared large block letters to introduce the theme. As we collect words and attach them to the block letters, this system provides an excellent way to sort words; each category on a different letter. We may sort by content words, by categories within the theme (e.g., in our *Indian Tribes* theme, each letter may contain words from different tribes), or by parts of speech, as this article describes.

The thematic word wall is an ideal instructional technique for having students look at one of the basic building blocks of writing—word choice. My students learn early in the year that using more descriptive words turns dull writing into stories that engage the reader's imagination. My class begins the process of writing by looking closely at word choice, and by studying the way in which words are used to write more descriptively. This, in turn, facilitates students to become more confident writers.

BUILDING THE WORD WALL

The word walls that we create in my classroom are not just lists of words. (We modify a technique that I learned in a workshop given by Kay Brallier [1996].) Index cards are arranged to spell out a word central to the topic the class is studying (e.g., FRIENDS, INDIAN TRIBES, WHO DONE IT?). Each letter of the theme word is made up of student-created cards on which words have been written. The words written on each card are collected from the students' background knowledge of the theme (e.g., when describing "mystery" characters, they may write *evil* and *hideous*; when thinking of description of "mystery" feelings, they may say *brave* or *embarrassed*). As they read, they collect additional words for the wall from their reading. When the wall is sorted by parts of speech, the students consider picking verbs for one letter, adjectives for another, and adverbs for a third. A border surrounds the large theme word and is made up of an alphabetical list of theme-related nouns with matching pictures. The entire word wall is 3 feet high and ranges from 15 to 20 feet long, depending on the length of the theme word. When students invest time creating such a word wall, they gain a sense of ownership, and they are more apt to use these words in their writing.

For the last quarter of the school year, the class selected MYSTERY? as the theme for the word wall. When beginning this word wall activity, students were instructed to choose primarily multisyllabic words, with the help of a thesaurus; in the beginning of the year, the students chose primarily one-syllable words. Adjectives, root words, and suffixes made up the inner letters, and nouns associated with a mystery were used to form the border. Students came up with words fitting each of the categories. *Instant Vocabulary* (Ehrlich, 1968) is a resource that my students use to assist them in finding words with certain affixes, or root words. Figure 2–1 shows the MYSTERY word wall. Each block represents a student-made word card. Figure 2–2 is an enlarged version of the letter M from our word wall. Figure 2–3 lists a sample

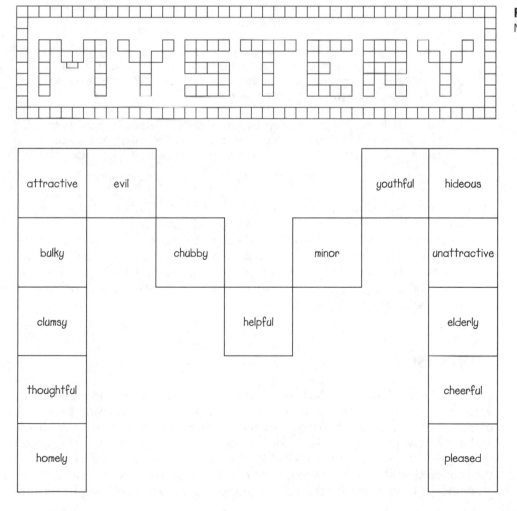

FIGURE 2–1 Sample Mystery Word Wall

FIGURE 2–2 Sample Letter M from the Mystery Word Wall

FIGURE 2–3 Mystery Word Wall Words

A sample of words chosen by students to mount on the word wall. (Each word is written by students on a card, then mounted on the designated letter.)

M—adjectives describing characters: attractive, bulky, cheerful, chubby, clumsy, elderly, evil, helpful, hideous, homely, minor, pleased, thoughtful, unattractive, youthful

Y—adjectives describing the setting: ancient, attractive, bustling, delightful, gigantic

S—adverbs: differently, excitingly, friendly, hopefully, lovely, peacefully, quickly, roughly, safely, slowly, smoothly

T—adjectives describing feelings: brave, depressed, disagreeable, downhearted, embarrassed, humiliated, mortified, melancholy, satisfied

E—adjectives describing a person's body: bald, considerable, healthy, mighty, slim, strong, tremendous, unhealthy

R—words having the suffix CIAN, which means having a certain skill or art: beautician, dietitian, electrician, logician, magician, mathematician, mortician, musician, optician, patrician, physician, pediatrician, pyrotechnician, technician

Y—words containing the root DUC, DUCE, or DUCT, which comes from the Latin *ducere*, meaning to lead: abduct, aqueduct, conductive, educate, introduction, product, reduce, reduction

Border—alphabetical lists of nouns related to a mystery: alligator, bridle, catfish, Dalmatian, ermine, fright, giant, helicopter, iguana, juggler, karate, letter, magazine, nicotine, octopus, peas, quicksand, racer, sickle, telephone, unicorn, vegetable, wreckage, x-ray, yawl, zodiac.

anaconda, brontosaurus, calumet, denture, enclosure, fireworks, gooseberries, hickory nuts, immortal, janitor, kingfisher, lobster, magnet, Napoleon, Oxford, paddle, quail, rascal, saxophone, tang, umiak, victim, wolf, X-Files, yacht, zero.

of words chosen by students to mount on the word wall. (Each word is written by students on a card, then mounted on the designated letter.)

Because we are collecting words from stories, textbooks, and other resources, not all words directly connect the word *mystery*. However, all can be used in the students' writings. For example, a student's mystery story may begin in an *ancient enclosure* with a *hideous magician* and an *elderly mathematician*. The word wall provides a source of new vocabulary for all students.

CONCLUSION

Building a thematic word wall has two purposes. First, I want to expand my students' vocabularies. Second, more importantly I want to give students a greater awareness of the words they already know so they can communicate their ideas more clearly and accurately. Learning five new words is far less meaningful than having better control over 100 words a student already knows at some level. At the beginning of the year, students frequently choose words from their everyday conversation. When students focus on increasing their use of adjectives and adverbs, their writing can improve dramatically using these words. Later in the year, I encourage my students to go a step further and use a thesaurus to attach a synonym to each of the word wall words; if a student chooses the word *abduct*, the synonym *kidnap* also goes on the word wall. Once students learn to use a thesaurus, a moment of magic occurs: Those 100 familiar words have expanded into many more words students are able to use in speaking and writing.

Several times a year, I ask my students how much they use the word wall in writing. Often their reply is "I don't use it very much at all." This response used to be discouraging. I did notice that a few words from the word wall appeared in their writing when I asked students to underline them in their writing. But once I looked at the overall increase in word variety and complexity, I realized that the process of creating these word walls is indeed having a greater effect on my students' writing than even they themselves know. My students have begun to think more about the words they are using.

Making thematic word walls is fun! And the resulting writing is fun. Once students begin expressing their ideas in writing and are successful at it, writing always comes more easily and is much more enjoyable for them.

REFERENCES

Brallier, K. (1996, August). *Back to basics with a twist*. Seminar presented in Fresno, CA.

Ehrlich, I. (1968). *Instant vocabulary*. New York: Simon & Schuster.

VOCABULARY BUILDING: SOMETIMES LESS IS MORE

Martha Dudley

Jessica, Jesus, Ricardo, and Heather stand at the bulletin board. The four students are teaching their classmates the word they've worked on for the Mayan word wall, and they're determined to get that word and its meaning across. Jessica's role was to letter the word on a sentence strip and present its spelling and punctuation. She's drawn the letters of the word hieroglyphic to look as if they were chiseled from stone, and she explains the connection between the word and the lettering style. Patiently she pronounces the word and spells it for those sitting farthest from the bulletin board; finally everybody has spelled it correctly on his or her vocabulary sheet. Now it's Jesus's turn. He's drawn a panel of Mayan glyphs, and he explains that some glyphs stand for sounds and some for words. Carefully copied from the frontispiece of a Mayan folktale, the glyphs effectively illustrate the meaning of the word. The listening students make quick sketches in the memory cue column of their vocabulary sheets, as shown in Figure 3–1. Then Ricardo takes over. He starts with the glossary definition from our social studies book, which he has printed on a sentence strip, adds information from the dictionary about the meaning of hiero and glyph, and concludes by defining the word as picture writing, which, although it doesn't convey the exact meaning of the word, is an approximation that his audience can remember.

Heather finishes the presentation with a riddle, also printed carefully on a sentence strip: "What is written with stone and not with a pen?" Students look up from their vocabulary sheets to applaud briefly as Team Four sits down. I sigh. Only seven more teams to go!

FIGURE 3–1 Vocabulary Collection Form

Vocabulary Unit: _____ Name _____ Date _____			
Vocabulary Word	Definition	Sentence	Memory Cue

REFLECTION: WORTH THE TIME IT TAKES

How many words are we learning in this way? Only 16. This isn't an arbitrary number; it's the number of teams in my morning and afternoon academic blocks, and each word represents work by four students.

I teach literature, language arts, and social studies to two groups of approximately 32 students in this academic block setting. My classes are heterogeneous, with reading scores ranging from well below the 10th national percentile to above the 80th. Over half of my students begin seventh grade with scores below the 50th percentile. The boundaries of my students' vocabularies are narrow and represent very closely the limitations of their knowledge and thinking. Consequently, I've tried many approaches to building vocabulary, believing that students cannot think about concepts for which they have no words.

Later, in the after-school quiet of my classroom, I look at the word wall. It is handsome: the different lettering styles; the illustrations created simply but effectively with colored pencils; and the variety of sentences, riddles, and Jeopardy-type questions combine to make it visually interesting. The word *elite* is lettered in classic Roman letters, illustrated by a huge stone head showing that the Olmec must have had both an elite and a group of commoners to create such monumental works of art, and defined in a student's own words as "The most powerful, respected and important people." *Astronomy* is conveyed through a drawing of our solar system, copied from an encyclopedia, and the riddle, "What do you get when you mix the sun, moon, and stars?" I reflect upon the several class periods it took to create the wall and the time it takes to present it. Again I assure myself that covering fewer words, and learning about and teaching those words to others in various verbal and graphic ways are worth the time it takes. If 16 new words do become a usable part of students' vocabularies, if they are words that help students understand important aspects of a historical period or culture, and if they are words that are useful in contexts beyond that particular social studies unit, the time is well spent.

The social studies word wall is one component of our work to broaden and deepen our well of words. Other components are the vocabulary sheets just referred to (see Figure 3-1) and a bingo game we play as we learn and review the words. Words from literature and spelling lists are added to the Mayan words over a 3-week period until we have 24, the number that fits onto a 5×5-inch square bingo card (the middle square is the free square).

A VOCABULARY UNIT, STEP BY STEP

One component of a vocabulary unit is a group of 16 social studies words. These are presented as a list, along with four tasks for each word (see Figure 3–2). Each group of four students works on one word, dividing the tasks among themselves. Students work on sentence strips and have copies of various lettering styles. I provide paper for illustrations, and students use their own colored pencils. When work is completed on all 16 words, I put up the word wall and each group of four students presents their word. As the students make their presentations, their classmates complete the vocabulary sheets.

In addition to the 16 social studies words, words from literature and spelling lists are chosen for the unit. We discuss some in the context of the literature from which they are taken, and the meaning and orthography of others are learned through our spelling lessons. Students complete vocabulary sheets with the correct spelling, definition, a sentence which conveys the meaning, and a memory cue, which may be a small drawing or a synonym.

FIGURE 3–2 Mayan Word
Wall Student Directions

Mayan Word Wall

1. archaeology/archaeologist
2. astronomy
3. codex
4. elite
5. hieroglyphic
6. fertile
7. literate
8. peninsula
9. priest-king
10. sacrifice
11. stele
12. terrace
13. tropic/tropical
14. pyramid
15. ceremony
16. mosaic

A. Print your word on a sentence strip, using an attractive and legible lettering style.
B. Draw and color a picture to show what the word means. (no white showing)
C. Print a definition in your own words.
D. Choice:
   Use the word in a sentence that shows what the word means.
   Write a "jeopardy" answer.
   Write a riddle.
   Can you think of something else to help your classmates learn this word?

Example: quetzal

Quetzals were valued by the Mayan and Aztec people because this tropical bird had beautiful long green tail feathers.
Answer: A Central American bird with brilliant green and red plumage and long tail feathers. Question: What is a quetzal (set)?
What is both a Guatemalan coin and a bird?

When we have 24 words, students write the words on two bingo cards. With vocabulary worksheets in front of them, and with my encouragement to help each other, we play several noisy sessions of Vocabingo. Sometimes, as we've gone through the unit, I've created a master set of vocabulary sheets from which I read definitions, sentences, and memory cues. More often, when the unit is complete, I borrow a good set of vocabulary sheets from a student, copy them, and use them in my role of bingo caller.

To finish our unit, we have to have a quiz. I provide a list of the 24 words, and students are instructed to number the lines on their own paper from 1 to 24. As I read each definition aloud, students choose the word from their list to write on their papers. We correct the quiz immediately in class, and we're ready to learn 24 more words!

ANIMAL, VEGETABLE, OR MINERAL 4

Carol Surabian

"Before we begin this chapter, turn to the review on page 216. Write the review words on a sheet of paper and find the definitions in the glossary."

Some of my students in the seventh-grade history class enjoy looking up words in the glossary, but many consider it a chore that does nothing to further their understanding of the text. This is usually expressed to me by the expression, "This bites!" For the most part, I agree with them. But I know my students cannot access the information in the text without a working definition of these vocabulary words. How best to help them as we work through the chapter?

I access my students' prior knowledge of a chapter in our history textbook by having them do a quickwrite. For 5 minutes, they write everything they know about the topic, as well as associations they may have to it. Some students know a lot, but many know little or nothing. I then give them a list of words that they will need to understand by the end of the chapter. I have them cut the words apart and sort them by *People*, *Places*, and *Things*. They work in groups of two or three and can argue among themselves as they try to sort out the words. Using the basic rules of grammar, I remind them that proper nouns (which are capitalized) name people and places, and that common nouns (lowercase) name things or people and places in general. I divide the class into thirds if the review list is exceptionally long, and each group is responsible for one-third of the words. Then I have them reorganize into three new groups. Each new group consists of one student who sorted the first third, one student who sorted the middle third, and one who sorted the last third. The "expert" student from each part then shares with the other two. This is called a "jigsaw."

We have discussions on how to tell if a word is a proper (specific) noun or common (general) noun. I reiterate that underlined or italicized words are usually titles of books. Placement in the sentence can also aid them in deciding what part of speech the word is. At the beginning of a sentence, the noun is used as a subject. In our text, this is usually a person.

PROCEDURE

For a unit on Islam, I might use words such as *Allah*, *Anno Hegira*, *Baghdad*, *caliph*, *Damascus*, *hajj*, *Mecca*, *mosque*, and *pillars of faith*. Using the sort, students decide which of these words belong in each category (see Figure 4–1). When they are finished, students begin to read the chapter. As they read, they can move a word to another

FIGURE 4–1 A Word Sort About Islam

PEOPLE	PLACE	THINGS
Anno Hegira	Allah	caliph
Mohammed	Damascus	mosque
(Allah)	Mecca	pillars of faith
(caliph)		hajj
		(Anno Hegira)
(Words moved during reading)		

FIGURE 4–2 Excerpt from a Student's Glossary

WORD	DEFINITION	SENTENCE
Anno Hegira	year of the flight	The first year in the Muslim calendar is 622, named Anno Hegira, or "Year of the Flight."

column if it is not correct. They may highlight the word if it is in the correct column. For example, many students misread A*nno* H*egira* as A*nna* H*egira*, placing it in the "People" column; it actually belongs in the "Things" column. They write short phrases or draw graphics (sketches) to help them follow the meaning. In the case of A*nno* H*egira*, they draw a small calendar.

As students read the chapter, they also use a sheet of lined paper and create their own glossary (see Figure 4-2). Using the whole page of lined paper, they write the word to the left of the pink line margin; this allows the students to study the words by folding the paper so the definitions are not visible. They write the definition from the text and record the sentence from which it came.

CONCLUSION

This activity can be used in math and science as well as in social studies. Whenever students are faced with reading a difficult content-area textbook, understanding the new vocabulary is essential. When students are allowed to first draw on background knowledge and make guesses about the meaning of the terms and then manipulate their guesses by resorting the words as they read through the text, their understanding of both the vocabulary and the content of the text becomes more clear.

DISASTROUS WORDS

Tamara Harritt

Students love to collect words that have meaning to them. If it is something daring or dangerous, then eighth-grade students will behave attentively. As I introduced a unit on natural disasters, the students' hands popped up immediately with accounts of personal incidents they wanted the others in this class to hear about. Everyone seemed to have been involved either in an incident or near one as it occurred. They wanted others to realize how dangerous the event was and, most of all, to relate how brave they felt the whole time. No fear!

PROCEDURE

1. Using *Scope*, a popular magazine available by subscription from Scholastic, as a springboard to the unit, the students read one issue that includes a play, which aired as a written-for-television movie. Students choose a character's part to read aloud, and other students follow along in their copies. Through this reading, students confront vocabulary related to earthquakes. I use a follow-up discussion to find out which students are having difficulty incorporating the correct vocabulary into their discussion.

2. Students break into groups of four and read the article by Robinson on earthquake safety tips. As one student reads aloud, the other three follow in their copies of the magazine and watch for specific words that refer to earthquakes. Another student is the scribe and makes a list of these words. A spokesperson for each group is responsible for reading the group's collaborative list to the class.

3. The students write each word from their list on a blank card. Through group discussion, they agree on an informal definition for each word. In addition, the students concur on sorting the words into categories by a common attribute or characteristic. Examples of categories include: effects of earthquakes, physical actions, rescues, emotions of victims, and the aftermath.

4. Each group of students puts the words on a word wall, which is a large piece of butcher paper folded into four columns. The columns each represent a category of words that are grouped together, and each group determines its own categories. Each student stands, reads the word aloud while showing it to the class, and tells why the group thinks it belongs in a certain category. The word cards are not yet glued in place until all are

FIGURE 5–1 One Group's Word Wall

Crumbled	Devastating	Emergency	Victim
Rubble	Disaster	Rescue	Death
Tremor	Deadliest	Shelter	Grief-sticken
Strongest	Decay	Ambulance	Helpless
Destroyed	Tragedy	Paramedics	Frantic
	Terrible	Search	Homeless
		Red Cross	Missing

FIGURE 5–2 Vocabulary Illustration

1. genuine

2. genuine-really what it is said to be]adj.

3.

The Red Cross People are genuine to their work.

Oxford American Dictionary pg 36

4.

in view. The class then looks over the categories; revision may be necessary as they discuss the commonality of the categories. Last, I assign a student or two to glue the cards. For Figure 5–1, the students explained that their categories, from left to right, were "Earthquake Descriptions," "Aftermath," "Relief Efforts," and "Victims."

Because students rarely use these words spontaneously in their writing, I suggest that each student choose one word to (1) spell correctly; (2) define, using a dictionary; (3) write in a sentence; and (4) illustrate. The activity is done on a piece of paper folded into quarters. These pages can be made into a class book (see Figure 5–2). The class book is one of the students' favorite choices during free reading time. Middle schoolers always enjoy reading their own work. Through these multiple exposures, it is more likely that students will begin to include the words in their own writing.

CONCLUSION

This activity proved to be excellent for vocabulary understanding. From the beginning of telling stories of disasters, through reading and finding new disaster vocabulary in the text, to applying the vocabulary to our own class book, students deepened their initial understanding of the terms and began using them in their speaking and writing. Their stories of bravery now had the vocabulary to make them both interesting and more detailed.

REFERENCE

Robinson, M. R. (1999). Aftershock: Earthquake in New York. *Scope*, 48(6), 6–13.

6

VOCABULARY CAROUSEL: A MERRY-GO-ROUND OF WORDS

Kathleen Markovich

Every once in a while, a teaching strategy pops into our brains out of pure necessity. Here we were just beginning John Steinbeck's *The Pearl* (1947), and I was already behind. With spring tests approaching, I knew we had to move along more quickly, yet I knew my ninth graders were going to stumble over some of the vocabulary in the next few chapters. I realized that to truly capture the words, we needed to spend time—but we didn't have any. Right there in class, the strategy burst open. I counted students, counted the words on my list, and we all went to work.

I call this strategy vocabulary carousel because what we end up with are vocabulary words and definitions taped all around the classroom and students moving around the room, merry-go-round fashion, collecting them. Though the strategy was an improvisation, I have continued to use it when time is short and the to-do list is long.

PROCEDURE

The following are the steps in creating the vocabulary carousel:

1. I give each student a legal-size sheet of white paper and a bright marker. Then I tell my students to get their copies of *The Pearl* and a dictionary.
2. I assign one vocabulary word per student—numbering the words in the order they appear in the chapter. I also give the page number where the word can be found. If there are more words than students, I give the extra words to the students who finish early. If there are more students than words, I assign some of the words to pairs of students or two words to groups of three.
3. On the sheet of paper, students use the bright marker to write the number for the word (the number represents the order in which the words appear in the chapter) and the word spelled correctly. I tell them to write neatly and fairly large. "Remember that we all have to be able to read your writing," I instruct them.
4. Next, the students read the page assigned to them until they find their vocabulary word. When they find it, they use their marker to copy the sentence that contains the word and underline the word. If the sentence is long, I tell them to copy five words before and five words after the word— enough to get the context.

5. After they have the sentence copied—with quotation marks, the vocabulary word underlined, and the page number on which the word is found—they look up the word in the dictionary and decide, from the context, which definition is the correct one. Then they neatly copy that definition.

6. I walk around the room to monitor the work and to help students select the correct definitions. This is important; I don't want students to be embarrassed for selecting incorrect definitions, and I don't want the entire class using those definitions.

7. As students finish, they tape their papers to the walls of the classroom—all around the room—in the order the words appear in the chapter. We start at the classroom door for word #1, then move clockwise around the room, taping on the chalkboard, the bookcase, the TV screen—any spot we can find.

8. Next, I tell students to get out a sheet of lined paper, write the heading *Vocabulary, Chapter 2* at the top, then number from 1 to 24 (or whatever is the total number of words), skipping a line between each number.

9. Students move to the walls and stand in front of a word. They write the word on the line that corresponds with the word's number. Everyone is in front of a word, copying the word and its definition—a student is at #1 and starting his or her list at #1; another student is at #2 and starting his or her list at #2, and so on. When they finish, they all move to the next number. They keep moving in a merry-go-round fashion until they have copied all the words and all the definitions. A class can move through 20 words in a 30-minute merry-go-round.

10. When they have all the definitions, students return to their seats. They keep their lists of words and definitions out, and they begin reading the chapter—with key words defined in the order in which they appear in the chapter.

11. I keep the words on the wall for reference while we are reading the chapter. Then I put them in a folder for absent students to copy when they return to class. If students are reading as homework, they have the definitions even if they don't have dictionaries at home. If students are reading in groups or as a whole class, they can stop at the designated words and read their definitions.

EXTENSIONS AND EXAMPLES

This strategy will work for students at many grade levels and in many curricular areas. Because this is a quick way for students to get many definitions, it does not lend itself to concept words that require an in-depth study to understand the many facts of the concept, such as *meiosis, nationalism,* and *bear market.* However, the strategy does work to help students with basic comprehension words. The words my class used for Chapter 2 of *The Pearl* are shown in Figure 6–1.

CONCLUSION

This merry-go-round strategy has many advantages. It works very well when time does not allow for a more in-depth study of the vocabulary that students will encounter in their reading. Because I teach a 90-minute block schedule, the strategy was especially helpful to get my freshmen up and moving around but in an orderly and purposeful manner in the middle of the period. After the movement, they quickly settle down to read. The strategy is very helpful for students who do not have

FIGURE 6–1 Vocabulary List for Chapter 2 of *The Pearl*

1. estuary	7. poultice	13. perceptible	19. reluctant
2. bow	8. remedy	14. deliberately	20. illusion
3. stern	9. unsubstantial	15. shrilled	21. deftly
4. mirage	10. strewn	16. tactful	22. writhed
5. optical	11. undulating	17. speculatively	23. subsided
6. bulwark	12. obscured	18. adhered	24. receding

dictionaries at home—they go home with vocabulary lists that will help them comprehend their reading homework. Through cooperation and collaboration, students save the arduous task of looking up 24 vocabulary words on their own. We save time and energy and have more time to read and discuss the chapter.

My students also learned the importance of writing neatly. As students were trying to copy definitions, they groaned and complained when they encountered indecipherable handwriting. A couple of students were told by their peers to recopy their work so it could be read, and the messy culprits complied without a word from me. We used this strategy one more time several chapters later, and all the students wrote in their best handwriting or printing. Messy handwriting that had been all right to give to the teacher all year was suddenly not good enough. We all learned a valuable lesson about writing so others can read our work.

REFERENCE

Steinbeck, J. (1947). *The pearl*. New York: Viking Press.

SORTING FOR SUCCESS

Laurie Goodman

"I already know this stuff, Mrs. Goodman," Chris announces before we begin reading our text. Four other hands go up, and the same phrase echoes throughout the classroom. I ask for a show of hands of students who are familiar with the content of the unit that we are studying. About a third of the students raise their hands, indicating that in fifth grade, they studied earth science, too. I am thrilled to have students who have some knowledge of the vocabulary that they are encountering during a unit, but being realistic, I know that they are at different levels of understanding. I also am aware that some students have no knowledge of the vocabulary we deal with in the unit. This is a perfect opportunity for me to allow my students to work in cooperative groups, discuss what the unit words mean to them personally, and examine how these same words relate to each other.

Our discussion occurs in a nonthreatening environment during a word sort. Word sorts can be done in several ways, depending on your objectives. Sometimes students sort words into categories the teacher has chosen; this is called a closed sort. In contrast, in an open sort, students evaluate the words for relationships and choose their own titles for the categories (Bear, Invernizzi, Templeton, & Johnston, 2004; Tompkins, 2004). When students work together to evaluate the words of a unit, they are able to stimulate meaningful word associations as they activate their background knowledge prior to reading a text.

PROCEDURE

I use word sorts after my students have had some exposure to the words. To begin, my students and I write vocabulary words on large sheets of chart paper posted in the classroom where everyone can see them.

Then I divide students into small groups and our word sort begins with each group of students having the same set of word cards. A typical list of words that each group might sort is shown in Figure 7–1. They examine the words and discuss their meanings and relationships. At this point, students decide which words have strong associations. They sort these words into groups and decide on a category for each group. Students may have as many as eight and as few as three categories. Sometimes as students work, they may find a few words that they are unable to make any associations with as they sort; these words are set aside until the whole class shares.

FIGURE 7–1 List of Earth Science Words for a Word Sort

hanging wall	fault – block mountains	rift valleys	stress
deformation	anticline	foot wall	fold
normal fault	compression	oceanic crust	magma
tension	syncline	shearing	fracture
reverse fault	molten rock	continental crust	earthquakes
lateral fault	temperature	fault	Earth

This open-sort format allows me to assess the knowledge level of my student groups, and it validates my students as directors of their own learning.

MAKING A CONNECTION

Experience with the words during the sort activity increases each student's knowledge of the word. As Nagy (1988) has stated, the three properties of effective vocabulary instruction are integration, repetition, and meaningful use. Word sorts incorporate all three of these properties.

In class, we extend our word sort activity to the word wall hanging in the classroom. Each group of students shares with the whole class the categories they have chosen and the words they placed in each category. As a class we find similarities among the choices in each group of students, which we apply to our word wall. The steps in making this connection are:

1. Groups of students share their categories.
2. Students discuss the similarities of the categories.
3. Students evaluate the choices and determine which categories are most useful.
4. Students vote as a whole class on the rearrangement of the word wall.
5. Students label main word categories in red.
6. One student leads the class in discussion as two other students sort the word wall according to the agreed-upon categories.

CONCLUSION

My students now have ownership of the words because of the open-sort activity; however, they are still in the process of reaching full concept knowledge of the words. As they continue through this process, they will continue to make connections as they expand their knowledge. They will reach a point when they view the words on the word wall differently because of their knowledge level. I know when this happens because students will recommend or suggest, "Mrs. Goodman, I know this stuff a lot better now, and our word wall needs to be re-sorted." These students often will lead the class in a second extended word sort of the word wall.

REFERENCES

Bear, D., Invernizzi, M., Templeton, S., Johnston, F. (2004). *Words their way: Word study for phonics, vocabulary, and spelling instruction* (3rd ed.). Upper Saddle River, NJ: Merrill/Prentice Hall.

Nagy, W. (1988). *Teaching vocabulary to improve reading comprehension*. Newark, DE: International Reading Association.

Tompkins, G. E. (2004). *Fifty literacy strategies: Step by step*. (2nd ed.) Upper Saddle River, NJ: Merrill/Prentice Hall.

VOCABULARY SQUARES

8

Faith Nitschke

An effective strategy I have found that promotes student learning is creating vocabulary squares. I have used this activity with seventh and eighth graders as well as with both GATE and regular sophomores. I like this activity because it allows students who may not otherwise "shine" in the classroom to display the connections they make as well as the clever ways they can devise to symbolize or illustrate a word. This activity promotes the following skills and/or modalities: following directions, precisely defining a word, symbolizing that meaning with a picture or symbol, engaging in a creative process and thinking "outside the box," and providing a study guide that appeals to both linear and nonlinear learners.

PROCEDURE

The steps in making vocabulary squares are as follows:

1. I select words to be studied using different methods, depending on what we are doing in the classroom at the time. If words are student-selected, as from a core novel, each student works with the word he/she has chosen, pending my approval. Otherwise, I distribute words so each student is responsible for one word.
2. I give each student a sheet with two 5-inch squares. Most students need two squares, one for the rough draft, one for the final copy. Note: Giving students smaller squares is too confining for a detailed and clean final copy.
3. I give these directions to students:
   a. Write firmly, using a *black* pen.
   b. Write the word at the top of the square.
   c. Write a short definition (1–8 words) at the bottom of the square.
   d. Write your name along the right margin.
   e. Draw a picture or symbol in center of the square that illustrates the word.
   f. Keep the sheet in pristine condition. (Figure 8–1 is a sample of students' vocabulary squares.)
4. I grade squares, making sure students have followed directions, have a good definition, and have created a picture that assists in comprehension. I return them to students if corrections need to be made. In my grading system, the completed square is worth 20 points: 5 points for each of the three features mentioned, in addition to a total of 5 points if the square copies well. If the student's finished copy is difficult to read, then he or she loses points.

FIGURE 8–1 Two Students' Completed Vocabulary Squares

5. When all squares are complete, I reduce the pages twice, at 64 percent the first time through, and at 77 percent the second time. Squares are now approximately $2\frac{1}{2}$ inches. I cut out squares and mount them on $8\frac{1}{2} \times 11$-inch paper; 12 per sheet. Then, I duplicate a set of all squares for each student.

6. I distribute packets of words to students for use as a study guide. I have each student explain his or her square to the class as part of the assignment. Five to seven words per day is a reasonable number; more than that, and the students stop paying attention. Students are required to connect their definition to their drawing as well as use the word in a sentence. If the word comes from a core novel, they are to read the sentence from the novel. These are usually brief and nonthreatening opportunities for students to teach their peers, an activity that allows even the shy child a relatively easy opportunity to speak in front of others. Students are appreciative of their peers' creativity and seem to enjoy hearing how and why they have depicted their word in the way they did.

The students now have a study for the vocabulary quiz I will give after all have shared. We repeat this activity throughout the year, and students add each new guide to their collection. After a word has been presented, it may appear on other quizzes later in the school year. Students constantly review the words until each becomes a part of their own spoken and written vocabularies.

CONCLUSION

I like this activity because it is student-centered. Students are responsible for the information they will share with their peers. I step out of the center and act as facilitator (and monitor). Studying from a group of pictures seems much more exciting than studying from a list of words and definitions. This method assists the student who is a visual learner. For other learners, they can focus on the definition instead of the image. Even though I went through school studying lists (which was a method that worked for me), I find that the students' drawings create in me a better intuitive feeling for words than I had before. I find that when I encounter one of the words from the students' sheets, my mind seems first to "grab" the image that a student has drawn and then I move to the written definition.

9

PARTS-OF-SPEECH WORD WALL

Cynthia J. Stovall

Students sit pondering a picture of an old farmhouse that is attached to a posterboard, and I ask them to think of words to describe the picture."I think it's spooky," Alyssa states as she writes her word, spooky, on the poster. Luis blurts out, "Haunted, I think it's haunted," as he adds his word to the poster. The students sit and discuss the picture, adding words and phrases to describe it. They continue to work until the poster is filled.

My special education students are brainstorming a list of words and phrases to assist them in adding detail to their stories. The posters are displayed around the classroom for the students to refer to while they write. The brainstorming and writing of words and phrases give the students a source to pull ideas from as they write. Many of my students have word-retrieval difficulties and cannot recall the words they wish to use. Also, students with special needs often do not recognize the conventions of grammar. Teaching conventions requires continual reinforcement.

Students choose words from their posters to make word cards for the parts-of-speech word wall. The words are placed on the wall according to their parts-of-speech category. The word card contains the word, its part of speech, and a sentence in which the word is used correctly. (A sample word card is shown in Figure 9–1.) The word is then added to the class' parts-of-speech word wall. During the year, the word wall becomes a resource for students to consult when they need a word.

PROCEDURE

First, we create descriptive posters, and then we make word cards and create a word wall. The steps we follow are:

1. The students look at pictures and then brainstorm descriptive words and phrases, which they then write on a poster.
2. I display the completed posters around the classroom and encourage students to use them as a resource for writing.
3. Students choose words from the posters to make word cards.
4. Students use their own knowledge or a dictionary to identify the part of speech of the word.
5. Students create a word card, listing the word, identifying the part of speech, and using the word properly in a sentence.
6. Students display word cards on the parts-of-speech word wall.

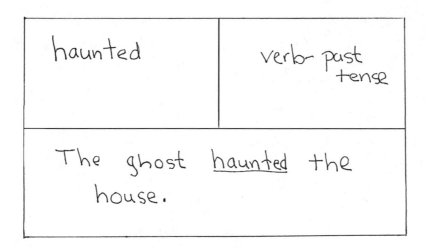

FIGURE 9–1 Student
Word Card

7. I use the "Word Art Gallery" in a word processing program to create the headings for the different columns on the wall, such as *noun, verb, adjective, negatives,* etc.

Words for the wall can be generated from all subjects that are being taught. However, all the words are sorted on the word wall by their part of speech. The word wall can be used during writing: When a student needs a prepositional phrase, for example, he or she can look at the preposition section of the wall as a reference to begin the phrase.

CONCLUSION

Topics for the activities can be generated from a science, history, math, or writing theme. The word wall reemphasizes grammar concepts that the students have been taught during the school year. As students revise their written work, a reference, such as the parts-of-speech word wall, assists them by inspiring ways to expand their work.

Exploring Definitions

Most of us have experienced a teacher who assigns a vocabulary list and asks the students to look up each word in the dictionary and write the definition. If teachers understand that students must do more than just copy a definition to learn a word, they might ask the students to use the words in a sentence. Although this traditional approach may have some positive results, especially for those who had some understanding of the words prior to the activity, researchers have learned that little real learning comes from such an activity. Nagy (1988) asserts that "definitions alone can lead to only a relatively superficial level of word knowledge" (pp. 4–5). One of the most obvious reasons for the failure of this approach is that dictionaries must give clear, concise meanings, not allowing for descriptions and uses beyond a phrase or two. Most words require much more in the way of explanation in order for students to understand meanings.

Beck, McKeown, and Kucan (2002) propose a viable alternative to copying dictionary definitions. They explain that when words are *described*, not *defined*, students are able to understand the word's relationship to other words in their background. Students then can discover a meaning through discussions and activities. When Marzano (2004) outlines his steps for vocabulary instruction, he encourages teachers and students to describe the vocabulary words. This is not to say that students should never use the dictionary. Quite the contrary. Some of the articles in this section show how teachers use the dictionary effectively with their students.

Although these activities introduce words through constructivist activities, students still have only a rudimentary understanding of the words. Laurie Goodman's article allows students to rate their understanding of words and chart their growth in understanding as they work with the words. Sara Silva also asks students to chart their growth in understanding as they use the word in a science experiment. They begin with a simple description and add to that as they read or perform the experiment. Cathy Blanchfield's vocabulary discussion encourages students to discuss the words within the context of the text and to build on what they already know about the word.

In Sarah Streib, Cathy Cirimele, and Carol Surabian's articles, students explore meaning by manipulating words for presentation and sharing. Joe Perez shares how he creates a toolbox of literary terms. They add the literary terms as they encounter examples in the texts, describing each term through the context in which it was encountered. Ann Brandon's idiom activity encourages all students, especially English learners, to describe the meanings of common idioms.

REFERENCES

Beck, I. L., McKeown, M. G., & Kucan, L. (2002). *Bring words to life: Robust vocabulary instruction.* New York: Guilford Press.

Marzano, R. (2004). *Building background knowledge for academic achievement: Research on what works in schools.* Alexandria, VA: Association for Supervision and Curriculum Development.

Nagy, W. E. (1988). *Teaching vocabulary to improve reading comprehension.* Newark, DE: International Reading Association.

WORD EXPERT

10

Sarah K. Streib

As we browse our selection for unfamiliar words before reading our new selection from Mrs. Frisby and the Rats of NIMH (O'Brien, 1971), I survey the sea of studious faces and ask, "Does anyone see a problem word in this selection that we should add to the board?" My students know that a problem word is a word whose meaning they do not know and that they are usually unable to pronounce. Before reading every selection, my students and I browse the first few pages to identify and discover some of those words and write them either on chart paper or on the chalkboard.

    Surprisingly, Roberto, one of my English language learners, raises his hand.

    "Thank you, Roberto. What is the word that you found?" Roberto normally does not share in class.

    "S-Q-U-A-W-K-I-N-G."

    "Excellent choice, Roberto. The word you have chosen is squawking," *I reply. "What do you think that word means?" I question.*

    "I don't know, but the next word in the sentence is loudly, *so it must be something that you do loudly," Roberto volunteers.*

    "Great use of context clues, Roberto," I proudly reply.

    Amy raises her hand next. "I found a word, Mrs. Streib," she interjects.

    "Yes, Amy. What is the word you found?"

    "Endangered. The endangered owl, having been hunted to the point of extinction, flew quickly away."

    "What do you think this word means?" I probe deeper. . . .

The discussion continues as a few more students share new vocabulary words. I may add a word or two to our list depending on how many words the students choose. We will use this list before, during, and after reading a selection to increase comprehension of the text, to assist students in integrating new words into their vocabulary, and to use the words in meaningful ways by utilizing the *Word Expert* strategy.

    Word Expert is a strategy in which students become knowledgeable about specific words. Students identify a word that is of interest to them and then throughout the reading process, they interpret, analyze, synthesize, and evaluate information about the word. The students create a poster of this information that will be shared when they teach the class about their word during a postreading activity.

PROCEDURE

The following is the procedure for becoming a *Word Expert*:

1. Before reading the selection, I list the words. Groups, pairs, or individual students choose one word to share. It is their responsibility to analyze, research, and discover information about this word.
2. Students begin by writing the word in the center of a piece of paper. They may choose to copy the sentence from which the word was taken or they may write what they think the definition is underneath the word. I encourage my students to "attack" their words using a variety of vocabulary skills including context clues, apposition, and word structure.
3. As we read the selection, students may revise their initial ideas. I explain that process, not product, is the most important thing. While reading the text, students are also analyzing their vocabulary word in context in order to discover which part of speech it is as well as if the word has a prefix, or suffix, or if it is a root word. They will add that information to the posters they are creating. Figure 10–1 shows how that poster might be organized.
4. After reading the selection, students are asked to add more information to their posters. At this point, students are invited to use writers' tools, such as a thesaurus and a dictionary, to deepen their understanding of the word. Students may add analogies, synonyms, antonyms, homographs, homophones, metaphors, multiple meanings, similes, personification, and etymologies to their posters. They may even choose to create a visual representation of their word and display that on the poster.
5. Finally, students share their word poster with the class.

Amy's poster on *endangered* includes the syllables, synonyms, antonyms, apposition, prefix, suffix, base word, part of speech, and new context for her word. Roberto worked with a group and chose to present the word *pasture*. His poster includes the context, the definition, a picture, and a new context for the word. Figure 10–2 is Roberto's group poster.

FIGURE 10–1 Sample Word Expert Poster

Syllables		Synonyms
Etymology		Antonyms
	Word	
	Definition from text	
Part of Speech		New Context

FIGURE 10–2 Roberto's Word Expert Poster

Pasture: a field for eating

pasture

When at length she came abreast of the barn, she saw the cattle wire fence that marked the other end of the pasture; and as she approached it she was startled by a sudden outburst of noise.

The green pasture was dotted with cows.

EXTENSION ACTIVITIES

I have used these posters as a springboard for an open or a closed sort activity. Students may sort their *Word Expert* posters with their classmates' posters, or I might give them assigned topics for sorting. This is great for visual learners. They may also write the word on one piece of paper and a synonym or two on another piece of paper and then match these up as a Concentration-type activity during center time.

CONCLUSION

The *Word Expert* strategy involves taking a word out of the context of a story and discovering its denotative and connotative meanings. It provides students with opportunities to explore a variety of related words, and also allows them to take ownership of a word at their level and to share their knowledge with other students.

REFERENCE

O'Brien, R. C. (1971). *Mrs. Frisby and the rats of* NIMH. New York: Simon & Schuster.

VOCABULARY SELF-CHECK

Laurie Goodman

I often discover a powerful teaching strategy the hard way. During an integrated social studies/language arts unit, I required my eighth graders to incorporate the significant unit vocabulary words in their performance projects. As soon as I explained the assignment, Josh's hand went up, and he said, "I'm not sure what some of these words mean. The dictionary definition doesn't fit what we are studying." That's when it hit me: Vocabulary development should be like turning up a dimmer switch—we all start out in low light; then as we progress through the unit of study, our conceptual vocabulary knowledge should increase to bright light. Josh's comment led me to learn more about teaching vocabulary and to change the way I teach it.

In-depth comprehension of a unit of study requires learners to fully understand the vocabulary of that unit. This development of vocabulary knowledge occurs throughout the unit. The levels of understanding, as stated by Baker, Simmons, and Kame'enui (1995), move from verbal association to partial concept knowledge into full concept knowledge. By the full concept knowledge, or "bright light," stage, students will be able to use the word and the concept in a meaningful way, such as in a performance project that involves complex writing. Having full concept knowledge means the student has the ability to extend the meaning of the word to related words and related concepts. Allen (1999) explains that at this level, students own the word and are able to analyze it and make connections with it to their lives and to the world.

CLASSROOM CONTEXT

Our journey to full understanding of the vocabulary related to the unit of study starts with students' awareness of their own level of word knowledge. Often my students believe that if they can read a word, they know its meaning. When I give them examples of the different levels of word knowledge through whole-class discussion, they realize that there are degrees of understanding in word knowledge.

At this point, I introduce the words that are significant to the unit we are about to study. I know that before students can begin reading the text, they will need to have some background knowledge about the subject and the vocabulary words that are part of the unit. We discuss the importance of being able to "own" the knowledge of the unit and identify their knowledge level as they examine each word on their list. These words will be posted on a word wall and used throughout the unit for the students to draw from as they experience various literacy activities.

PROCEDURE

1. Before students begin reading a new section of the text, I pass out copies of the vocabulary self-check chart shown in Figure 11–1 and students write the vocabulary words in the left column. In the other five columns, students rate their knowledge level and write an example and a definition of the word, if they can. As students examine each word and evaluate their knowledge level, they rate themselves with a plus sign (+), minus sign (−), or a question mark (?). If they put a plus sign on their chart in the column next to a word, they must be able to fill in the "Example and Definition" columns. This chart serves as an assessment tool for the students and me before we begin an in-depth study of a subject. I copy this chart and keep the copy until the end of the unit.

FIGURE 11–1 Vocabulary Self-Check Chart

Name _____

Vocabulary Self-Check

	Word	+ Example & Definition	? Example or Definition	− No Example or Definition	Example	Definition
1						
2						
3						
4						
5						
6						
7						
8						
9						
10						
11						
12						
13						
14						
15						
16						
17						
18						
19						
20						

Procedure:
1. Examine the list of words you have written in the first column. These words are related to the unit that we are about to study.
2. Put a +, ?, or − sign in the appropriate column.
3. If you put a + sign, fill out the example and definition columns of the chart.
4. Your example and definition must relate to the unit we are studying.

This chart will be used throughout the unit. By the end of the unit, you should have the chart completely filled out. You will find that you will be erasing and adding more precise information to your chart; therefore, write in pencil. This chart will be your pre- and postassessment check of the vocabulary of the unit of study.

2. Students revise their charts as they begin reading their text. They increase their level of understanding as they see the words in context and related to the concepts presented in the text. Students write in pencil so they can revise their examples and definitions as they progress through a unit. Students also draw information from their chart as they participate in literacy activities throughout the unit.

3. The chart then acts as a postassessment measure for the students and me as we compare their final chart to the copy of their prereading chart and reflect on their journey into in-depth word knowledge.

CONCLUSION

I am amazed at the difference this activity makes in my students' level of understanding with units that cover several content areas. The greatest benefit that carries over to their other classes is their awareness of their level of understanding when they really own a word in depth.

REFERENCES

Allen, J. (1999). *Words, words, words: Teaching vocabulary in grades 4–12.* York, ME: Stenhouse.

Baker, S. K., Simmons, D. C., & Kame'enui, E. J. (1995). *Vocabulary acquisition: Curricular and instructional implications for diverse learners* (Technical Report No. 13). Eugene: University of Oregon, National Center to Improve the Tools for Educators.

Vocabulary Discussions in Literature Circles

Cathy Blanchfield

"Here's one. How about the word purled?*" Martin suggested.*

"Aw, we know what that word means. It's the white thing you put into rings and necklaces," Juan suggested.

"Not that kind of pearl. That's spelled p-e-a-r-l. Here it has to do with the ocean. The sentence says, 'He pointed down at the wake that purled and foamed behind us as though a razor had slit the dark surface of the sea and allowed its mysterious light to shine through.' I think it means that the wave rose. That's my guess. Let's look it up."

Jennifer, always a step ahead, already had. "Purl: gold or silver thread or wire for embroidering or edging."

Martin kept the discussion going. "Read on. That's not the meaning that fits in this sentence."

"Oh yeah," Jennifer found it, "here it is. Purl: a gentle murmur or movement (as of purling water)."

This is a typical discussion in my classroom during literature circles. Students choose books from a variety of titles centered on a certain theme; the ones who chose the same title are grouped together. This discussion took place during a vocabulary collection time with a group of students reading Paula Fox's *The Slave Dancer* (1973).

Kids, especially adolescents, need choice. So much of the curriculum is chosen for them, but as a teacher, I am constantly searching for ways to encourage my students to take charge of their own learning. Wlodkowski and Ginsburg found in their 1995 study of motivation that to "encourage students to make real choices (in content and assessment methods) based on their experiences, values, needs, and strengths" develops positive attitudes toward learning (p. 119).

PROCEDURE

During readers' workshop, students choose many of their learning activities, including vocabulary. Each week, the students decide on three words to learn. They are charged with choosing words that are important to the understanding of the story and words that most members of the group do not understand. As Martin, Juan, and Jennifer negotiated meaning, they discussed multiple meanings, contextual clues, and dictionary definitions. Together they deepened their understanding

FIGURE 12–1 Student
Vocabulary Handout

READERS' WORKSHOP

VOCABULARY ACTIVITY

As you read, you will come across words that you do not know. Ask your group about these words. If the majority of the group does not know your word choice and it is important to the story, this is a good word for your group list. Each week, your group needs to decide on 3 words that you all want to learn. Each of you will complete the following for every word:

1. Copy the sentence from the book that contains the word.

2. Discuss the meaning of the word with your group. Now write the meaning of the word—this may be from the dictionary, but write it in your own words. The purpose is to understand the word! You may all write the same meaning in your journals.

3. Use the word in your own sentence. Be sure that you use it correctly. Talk with each other first. Do not write the same sentence as other members of your group. Each group member needs a different sentence. Underline the word in your sentence.

4. Each time you use one of your group words in your own writing, underline it. This will be part of your assessment at the end of the novel.

5. As a group, display your words on the wall.

---

of the word *purl*. As a group, they copy the sentence from the book and write their negotiated meaning for the word. Then, individually, students each use the word in their own sentences. The sentence from the book serves as a model sentence for their own sentences. The more creative students will see how it is used and create a totally different context; the more limited students will change only a few words of the original sentence. I give credit when the students use the vocabulary words in journal entries and process writing pieces written during the readers' workshop unit. The students who have a clear understanding of the word will use it fluently. In this way, I check the students' depth of understanding. Students receive a handout explaining this procedure at the beginning of the workshop session (see Figure 12–1).

CONCLUSION

If time permits, each group of students makes a word strip with the word and its definition for our word wall. Some of the more self-directed groups add all of their words to the wall. Some groups add only a few. By the end of the novels, our walls are filled with words. Kids share the words with each other and use words from other groups in their writing.

REFERENCES

Fox, P. (1973). *The slave dancer*. New York: Dell.
Wlodkowski, R., & Ginsburg, M. (1995). *Diversity and motivation*. San Francisco: Jossey-Bass.

Using Computer Software Tools to Expand Vocabulary

Carol Surabian

"I'm Nobody!" by Emily Dickinson, found in our anthology Elements of Literature *(1997), is one of my students' favorite poems. When asked why, many of them look at me as if to say, "Duh! It's short." It is true that brevity and seemingly simple language appeal to them. However, when pressed further to explain what they've read, students are lost.*

As we look at the poem, I ask about the word banish. *Joey in the back cracks, "Isn't that some deodorant?" The class erupts in laughter just as Joey knew they would.*

"No," I reply, "but if you take it apart, you find it contains the word ban. *Can you tell me what that means?"*

After some negotiation, we decide on a working definition. While most of the class is with me, Joey and his crew are in the back, creating some lessons of their own. They have learned that if they sit back, the rest of us will do the work and they can then write down the "right" answers. I need to pull that crew into the learning circle from the beginning and the computer lab creates the magnet.

PROCEDURE

My students have access to a computer lab about once every eight days. On our next visit, I pair up the students and have them go through the poem again, selecting words they need to clarify to create meaning. I let them log on to dictionary.com to find the definitions. From there they select the definition that best fits the context of the poem.

The teams use Microsoft Word to type in the poem or selection they will be working on. Each team creates a folder on the schoolwide server into which they will save the poem and all the links. Then the partners create a new page for each word they will define. They type or copy, cut, and paste the words and their definitions. This does not ensure understanding, however. Many times before they have copied copiously from the dictionary without much, if any, understanding. Therefore, after writing the definition, they need to add a sentence or two to explain the definition. The vocabulary page is then saved into their folder. When all words have been defined, the folder will have a document for the poem and one for each defined word.

Going back to the poem page again, I have them set up links to each vocabulary page. (See the list on how to create links and meaning.) When I click on each underlined word in the text, their definition and example of the word used in their own sentence comes up (see Figure 13–1).

I ask the students to create their folder for this activity on the student server at our school so other students can access their page and see what meanings they have discovered. They can compare their meanings with others in small groups of

FIGURE 13–1 Poem and Links

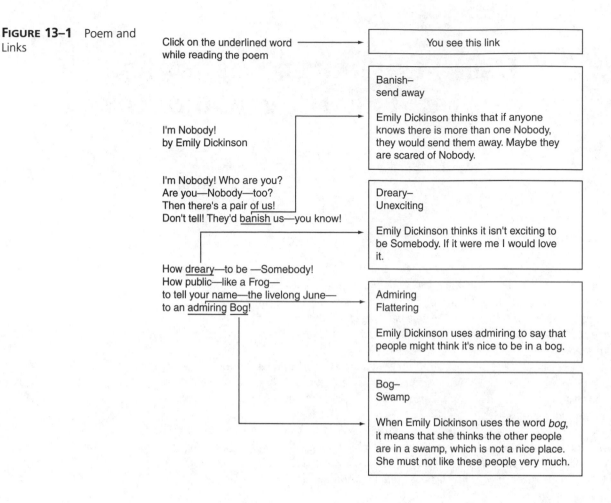

four or six. Partners can be sent to different groups, like a jigsaw, to explain the process they went through to come to that meaning. Folders can also be saved onto a disk or network system. The goal is for the students in the class to access to all the other groups' work.

These are the steps my students use to create the links:

1. Open a new document in Microsoft Word.
2. Type in the text of the poem and save it into a folder created for this activity.
3. Open Microsoft Word and type a word to be defined.
4. Open the thesaurus under *Tools* or log on to a dictionary site on the Internet.
5. Select a definition to write onto the vocabulary page.
6. Explain how the meaning fits the poem under the definition.
7. Save the vocabulary word document into the folder.
8. Return to Microsoft Word and open a new page.
9. Repeat steps 3–7 for each word the students wish to define.
10. Return to the poem page and highlight a word in the text that is defined.
11. Go to *Insert* and choose *Hyperlink*.
12. Open the document that matches the word you want and click link.
13. Repeat steps 10–12 for each of the words defined.

CONCLUSION

This strategy is better suited to short pieces or to a portion of a longer poem or story. Students need to scan or type in the selection before they can begin. However, some reluctant students find the opportunity to "play" on the computer to be the motivating factor; they are willing to choose the words they truly struggle with in order to have time on the computer.

In the past, I have viewed the computer in sort of a love–hate relationship. I love the fact that students can revise so easily on a word processor that they approach the activity willingly. I hate the fact that students would rather play games on the computer than read a book. This strategy of combining what is possible on the computer with a piece of reading is the start of a new relationship for the computer and I.

REFERENCES

Lexico Publishing Group, LLC. (2006). *Dictionary.com*. *http://dictionary.reference.com*.

Elements of literature. (1997). Austin, TX: Holt, Rinehart and Winston.

14

LITERARY TERMS

Joe Perez

One of the frustrations of English teachers is deciding what vocabulary to teach and how to do it. Certainly learning new words in reading context is fundamental. But beyond that lies another essential source of vocabulary—literary terms, such as *personification*, *imagery*, and *denouement* that are defined in most literature books.

By the time students are in their last two years of high school, they understand the definitions of most of these terms, and they might even be able to write glossary definitions for many. However, as Janet Allen (1999) points out, we understand words at multiple levels; just knowing a glossary definition is not enough to be able to use these terms in literary analysis and college entrance assessments. As high school teachers, we need to give our students multiple experiences with the terms so that their understanding deepens to what Allen (1999, p. 13) describes as "full concept knowledge," or the ability "to integrate the concept into meaningful use."

THREE DEVELOPMENTAL AREAS

Starting the beginning of the school year with these literary terms or *tools* will have long-term benefits. From my teaching experience, I find that the process of learning involves three areas: repetition, usefulness, and student ownership of the word. For example, I teach a chronological survey course in British literature and composition, and *Beowulf* comes up very early. Here is the opportunity to teach *epic* and *archetype*. Soon after comes the line "when night has covered the earth with its net." Is *personification* in the house?

As we wend our way through our epic *Beowulf*, I refer often to these literary tools and eventually students do, as they, too, naturally assimilate these words. This familiarity gives students a sense of expertise when they can use the more specific word *epic* instead of *poem* or *story*. Through repetition, not memorization, students begin to make bridges from words on the page to thoughts formulating in their brains.

Students begin to see the usefulness and facility of knowing these terms when they can use them as a sort of shorthand to focus their meaning when writing or talking about *Beowulf*. Later when they read from *Paradise Lost* or *Rime of the Ancient Mariner*, the word *epic* ties these works together. Students can consider what characteristics each of these works have in common. For example, both are great undertakings with an element of the supernatural. Both sweep the readers into places they have never experienced. Both challenge the readers on a philosophical level. E*pic*, then, is a powerful word that should not be overused or used incorrectly.

Once the students become familiar with literary terms, they begin looking at literature with this additional perspective. M*etaphor* and *simile* become much more relevant. After a few months, students begin looking at poems for *assonance* and *consonance*; they get that tick-tock of *iambic pentameter* in their bones. They begin to see the intricacies of the poet's craft. Perhaps in their own writing they can consider *irony* or *connotation*. And when the teacher, giving them group time to discuss the poetry they have studied, hears *ode* or *epiphany* bandied naturally about by students, it is a gratifying moment. The teacher can reasonably assume that students have taken ownership of the literary tool and will make it part of their life because it has been proven valuable and, for some, indispensable.

ALTERNATIVE METHOD

Now teachers can present these literary terms as they come along in their readings as described here. Or they can simply start with the "A" words in the text glossary and assign them 10 per week, for example. Perhaps some skipping around is in order. For instance, in my text, *alexandrine* appears first; however, I hold off on introducing that word until spring when Percy Shelley demonstrates its meaning. But *allegory*, *alliteration*, and *allusion* follow and are too juicy, too valuable to pass up. You may not encounter examples of these words immediately in the text, but that's okay; assign them anyway. Sooner or later the words will show up. When they do, I prompt the students to think about terms and discover which one is exemplified by the text at hand. And the students will experience the delicious shock of recognition.

When introducing these terms to the students, be enthusiastic; choose words that are mind-boggling whenever possible. For instance, *deus ex machina* is a great term! "God from a machine." What a compelling image and idea! How can a curious student possibly not want to delve into what it means and from whence it comes? I tell my seniors to be sure to use *deus ex machina* in their first college English class discussion. It will leave some impression.

EXTENSION

Students need to know that these terms exist in the everyday world. For example, when the president speaks of a T*rojan horse* strategy, students should be able to recognize this as an allusion to the I*liad*. A graphic organizer activity called a *Literary Tool Box* (see Figure 14–1) can be a great review activity, especially if students share their findings with each other. Students are asked to explain when and where they notice authors or speakers using examples of specific literary devices. In their *toolbox*, they keep a record of the terms and how authors, including themselves, use these devices. More reinforcement! It can be a regular weekly class activity or given for extra credit. Book and movie reviews from newspapers and literary magazines will provide rich sources of literary terminology.

EVALUATION

Weekly or bimonthly testing on these terms is optional. I believe that over nine months, diligent students will incorporate these words naturally into their own evaluative writing, but I do give them quizzes to monitor their degree of understanding. The quizzes are usually sentences or short paragraphs in which students show their

FIGURE 14–1 Literacy
Tool Box Review

Literary Term	When did you see it used? How? Where?	When have you used this literary term? In writing? In talking?

knowledge of definition and example. For instance, when I ask for a sentence show-ing personification, a student writes, "Shelley uses personification when he has the voice of the West Wind awaken the Mediterranean Sea." Or with *epic*, "Dickens wrote an epic about two great cities struggling with problems of justice and survival."

CONCLUSION

As students discover the use of literacy devices and work to use them, their under-standing of the terms deepens. Most, if not all, of these words could find their way to an SAT verbal exam. Certainly Golden State and AP examiners expect knowledge and use of these terms. And they will be used in numerous future contexts: college textbooks, movie and book reviews, and untold numbers of discussions about art and life.

REFERENCE

Allen, J. (1999). *Words, words, words: Teaching vocabulary in grades* 4–12. York, ME: Stenhouse.

VOCABULARY TEA PARTY

Cathy Cirimele

Making vocabulary an interesting and engaging experience for students is an ongoing challenge for any teacher. With the emphasis on vocabulary development in the English/language arts standards of many states and in the subsequent norm-referenced and standards-based assessments students are asked to complete, it becomes even more important to sometimes teach vocabulary in isolation rather than in context. In my composition classes this is also an issue, because the writing that students encounter at that level is more sophisticated and mature than what they might read in their free-reading novels. In addition, at any level, there is the awesome task of preparing students to face vocabulary that may be presented in short sentence excerpts or in analogies.

Regardless of the level, teaching vocabulary effectively is a pressing issue. If I can get students to engage in the process of discovering what words mean and the different ways in which they might be used, I can help them with the basic problems of recognizing denotation, connotation, and multiple meanings. With the emphasis on high-stakes testing, knowing what words mean and the different ways in which they might be used is vitally important. Finally, and even more important, the challenges of vocabulary are presented to them in all good literature as well as on tests.

Like many teachers, I have tried a variety of strategies to teach students vocabulary, both in isolation and in context. Vocabulary tea party is a variation of a strategy that I have begun using to encourage students to share their insights about literature. In one of those teacher moments that sometimes seem to come from nowhere, I adapted it to fit as a vocabulary lesson.

PROCEDURE

I begin by passing out 5 × 7-inch note cards, which immediately catch the students' attention. For some reason, they aren't used to writing in a small space. Of course, I am very mysterious about why I am giving them the cards. When I give them five cards each, they are even more intrigued. The next step is to give each student a vocabulary word. Which words I choose depends on my goal: I may choose vocabulary words from something we are going to read as a prereading activity, or I may simply choose words from a word list; for example, I sometimes use this lesson to acquaint students with the kind of vocabulary they might see on a list of words frequently found on the PSAT or the SAT.

The task is for students to write the word on a card, look up its meaning, use it in a sentence, and then make an illustration that demonstrates that they know what the word means. They can draw the illustration or cut out pictures from a

Figure 15–1 A Word Card for Vocabulary Tea Party

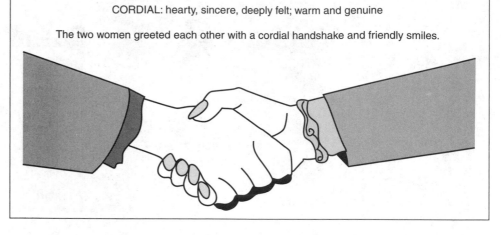

CORDIAL: hearty, sincere, deeply felt; warm and genuine

The two women greeted each other with a cordial handshake and friendly smiles.

magazine; however, many students choose to find pictures on my classroom computers or on their computers at home, or use the graphics on a computer. I always have a collection of magazines in my room. A sample vocabulary card is shown in Figure 15–1. After they finish this task, they exchange their cards with classmates. They circulate around the room to find four other students with whom they want to exchange cards. They share their card and then copy the word cards of four other people, sketching the illustration. At the end of 10 or 15 minutes, they return to their seats with five completed vocabulary cards.

During this process, students are required to explain their word to four classmates. If they are unclear about the meaning of the word or the way they used it in a sentence, this becomes apparent as they exchange cards. Students are not afraid to question each other and pursue a line of inquiry before they copy the card because they know that they will be responsible for the correctness of the information when they turn in the cards to me. I remind students that they will be graded accordingly, and if they don't understand a word or the way that it is used, they need to make sure they continue their inquiry until they do understand.

As a conclusion to this activity, I often ask each student to share an interesting word card with the rest of the class; they may share the word they were assigned or any other word card they found interesting. This serves as a vocabulary review session without actually having a test. Finally, students staple the five word cards together and turn them in. I quickly review the cards and usually give points based on the accuracy of the information. If students do not receive full credit, I remind them that it is their responsibility to check the word card for accuracy before turning it in. As a final review, the word cards can be posted on a word wall in the classroom.

CONCLUSION

This assignment is almost always successful for several reasons. It allows students to get up out of their desks and move around and talk to each other without someone reprimanding them about the noise level in the class. The word card exchange forces students to verbally explain their word. If a student they are exchanging with is confused, it becomes their task to clarify the word's meaning. Because it is a nonthreatening activity, students are more willing to tackle complex vocabulary words that have multiple meanings.

This truly is one of my favorite vocabulary assignments. It is great for Fridays, minimum days, or any day when something of consequence should be taught but socializing seems to be the priority. I repeat it a few times each year. After the first time, students always look forward to participating again. Just like any tea party, this one offers the opportunity to accomplish serious business while conversing and exchanging pleasantries. Jane Austen would be proud.

WHATEVER FLOATS YOUR BOAT: TEACHING IDIOMS TO ENHANCE READING AND ORAL COMPREHENSION

Ann Brandon

I was in a college literature class where the professor was dissecting a poem to death and I wanted to ask the off-the-wall question, "Could it be possible that the author did not have an underlying meaning and the words that are written mean just what they say?" However, I didn't want to make waves so I just figured that was the way the ball bounced and continued listening. We use idioms in our everyday speech and writing; we read idioms in literature, magazines, and newspapers and we hear them in television shows, movies, and in music. For students who are learning English, however, idioms can be confusing and hinder both reading and oral comprehension. Native English speakers also have difficulty navigating the meanings of some of the idioms scattered through communication.

Because the English language is replete with idioms, I thought exposing students to the mystery of idiomatic expressions would be a strategy to build both their reading and oral comprehension abilities in a way that might tickle their funny bones.

PROCEDURE

I begin the unit and in order to build up interest in studying about words and phrases, I enlist the help from my students' own speaking. As a class, we brainstorm phrases that they use in their own everyday conversations. Some of my students' examples are very contemporary: "dropped the dime" which means to tell on someone, "all up in my grill" which means being in someone's face or business, and "straight up" which can simply mean the adverb *totally*. We talk about these phrases, their evolution over time, and how some just drop out of the vocabulary and when brought up they are considered silly. This discussion allows students to think about how words and phrases are formed. I often ask the students to create a "teenage" slang dictionary, which increases my teenage awareness and serves as a guide for phrases that they can no longer use in their writing.

Next, I use 3 × 5-inch note cards and write an idiom such as "spilled the beans" or "up a creek without a paddle" on each card. When the students enter the classroom, I hand each one a card. The students then write their own guess on the back of the card as to what they think their idiom means. At this point I do not allow them to share with any partners. After each student writes a guess, we discuss that the term *literal* means leading to the next step. Once the students understand the meaning of *literal*, I give them a blank sheet of paper, colored pencils/markers, and have them draw a picture of their idiom's literal meaning.

After students finish their idiom's literal illustration, I hang the drawings around the room and give each student a stack of sticky notes. Next, the students participate in a gallery walk, looking at each idiom's illustration and writing on the sticky note what they think the figurative definition of the idiom is and then posting this definition on the illustration. In a class of 35 students, I will have the students go to only five or six of the illustrations. After this is completed, the owner of each idiom illustration takes it and matches the definitions from the sticky notes with his or her own from the beginning of this process. At this point the "guess" definition can be revised. Sometimes the students are able to determine the true meaning of the idiom based on the picture or on prior knowledge.

When the "guess" definitions are all recorded on the illustration poster, the students then look in a dictionary of idioms or online to find the figurative definition. I use a variety of books, but two of the most common are *Dictionary of Idioms* (Terban, 1996) and *Why You Say It: The Fascinating Stories Behind Over 600 Everyday Words and Phrases* (Garrison, 1992). Once found, they write the definition on their illustration poster. If they still have difficulty understanding it, I explain it to them.

At this point I explain to the students what an idiom is, how it is figurative language, and how authors in many mediums (novels, plays, movies, music) use idioms for creative and comical purposes. Students often get frustrated and ask why people can't just say what they mean. Now the shoe is on the other foot I tell them. I proceed to bring them back to the "teenage" phrase dictionaries they created earlier in the unit and ask the same question. With this many smiles appear and the students seem to understand the purpose of using idioms. Once the students have an understanding of their idiom's figurative meaning, they share it with the class. Figure 16–1 is an example of one student's idiom illustration.

Finally, to get a deeper understanding, I have the students write brief scenarios, mini-stories, or a fable for their idioms. Many of the idioms lend themselves to

FIGURE 16–1
One Student's
Illustrated Idiom

being lessons learned. For example, for Lorena's idiom, "don't bite off more than you can chew," she writes:

> Once there was this really shy girl named Mary who really wanted to be popular. She had many friends, but because she was so shy she stayed away from clubs and activities that were at school. Mary worried about this and her mom told her that she needed to focus on her school work instead of her desire to be popular. As the new school year started Mary decided that she would go ahead and join clubs and try out for a sport. She didn't tell her mother this because she was afraid she wouldn't be allowed. When club day came, Mary signed up for the spirit club and the science club. She even tried out for volleyball and made the JV team. Mary was so excited she made the team she couldn't wait to tell her mom even though she knew her mom wouldn't be happy. Mary begged her mom to let her stay on the team and she promised that she would still get good grades. Mary's mom agreed, but warned her that she would check on her grades every two weeks.
>
> As the semester went on, Mary's classes got a lot harder. She had more homework than ever in her classes, especially English. Her volleyball team had practice every day and games at least twice a week. She was also in the spirit club and had to help make posters and signs for the school's activities. Mary's grades began to drop and she begged her teachers to let her turn in work late. The grades were already sent home and Mary knew that when her mom got the grades she would be in trouble. When Mary got home, her mom was waiting for her with the report card in her hand. Mary immediately began to cry and ran to her mom crying, "I bit off more than I can chew!" Her mom gave her a hug and told her that they would work it out.

Lorena's story shows that she understands her idiom. Students share their stories within groups of four and then volunteer to share with the whole class.

CONCLUSION

Familiarizing students with idioms helps their reading and oral comprehension because they become more aware of language and how figurative language is a part of our everyday culture. After this unit it is fun to hear the students use these idiomatic expressions in conversation and they pick up on the expressions that I use in class on a regular basis. Teaching students to look for and understand idioms helps them understand literature better. For example, in Act 5, Scene 3 of *Romeo and Juliet* (Shakespeare, 2004), as Paris is about to visit the Capulet tomb, he instructs his page to listen closely for any sound or anyone approaching by saying, "Holding thine ear close to hollow ground." Although the students didn't automatically say, "That's an idiom," they paused at that line knowing that it meant something. Based on the context of the scene, they were able to come up with the correct response. So, if you're at the end of your rope, have your students play with the language of idioms because you will be tickled pink.

REFERENCES

Garrison, W. (1992). *Why you say it: The fascinating stories behind over 600 everyday words and phrases*. Nashville, TN: Rutledge Hill Press.

Shakespeare, W. (2004). *Romeo and Juliet*. Logan, IA: Perfection Learning Corporation.

Terban, M. (1996). *Dictionary of idioms*. New York: Scholastic.

17

USING MEANINGFUL CONTEXTS TO UNDERSTAND SCIENCE VOCABULARY

Sara Silva

Students in a content area, such as chemistry, often come across words that are unfamiliar to them. They are exposed to terms in the science classroom that are almost like a foreign language. Unless students use the words repeatedly and in meaningful contexts, they are useless or will have little significance for students.

Many students remember a word better if they are able to "see" it in addition to reading and hearing it. According to Blachowicz and Fisher (2002), students learn words best in meaningful contexts; however, students might need multiple exposures to the words before they know them well enough to use or remember them. I believe that over time and by repeatedly hearing and seeing them, students learn and remember the words as they use them in laboratory experiments and in writing assignments.

I have developed a vocabulary activity to be used in a science classroom in which students are exposed to new terms several times and in a variety of ways. They hear the words, read text where the words are used in context, discuss the words in groups, look up the words in the science textbook glossary, and finally complete an experiment or laboratory observation activity where the terms are applied to concrete objects. In this manner, new concepts will be easier to understand. As a final assessment, students write a short explanation of the experiment and the concept they now comprehend using the new terms they have learned.

PROCEDURE

The following steps give students multiple experiences with new science vocabulary:

1. Students write the vocabulary words in the first column of the Science Vocabulary Worksheet (see Figure 17–1). The teacher pronounces the terms and the students repeat them before writing them.
2. Students indicate their degree of understanding by marking 1, 2, 3, or 4, according to the key on the bottom of the worksheet, in the "Before Reading" column. At this point, there has been no discussion of the words.
3. Students silently read a text selection containing the new words; then they mark 1 to 4 on the vocabulary worksheet in the "After Reading" column, again indicating their degree of understanding of these words.
4. Working in groups of three to five, students share and discuss their knowledge of the words and complete the "After Discussion" column.

Science Vocabulary Worksheet

Word	Definition	Before Reading	After Reading	After Discussion	After Experiment or Observation

KEY
1: understand and can explain
2: understand, but can't explain
3: fuzzy
4: don't know

FIGURE 17–1 A Student Science Vocabulary Worksheet

5. Students fill in the "Definition" column at this time with a group-negotiated definition. If any words are unclear at this point, students look them up in the glossary.
6. Students share the definitions they have for each of the terms with the class, and the teacher clarifies any terms, if necessary.
7. Students complete a laboratory experiment that illustrates the terms. The teacher should emphasize the new terms, reminding students of their meanings, while going through the laboratory procedure and directions.
8. Students mark 1, 2, 3, or 4 in the last column, "After Experiment or Observations," again indicating their degree of understanding. Not all students mark a 1 in this column for each word, but each student realizes by now that their understanding for every word has improved.
9. Students produce a quickwrite, where they write an informal note to a friend (in another chemistry class) about what they did in class. They are to use all of the new terms correctly to explain the activity to their friend. It is at this time that the students see how their understanding has grown through this activity.

VARIATIONS

Students could write a poem, a short story, a paragraph, an advertisement, a newspaper article, or a comic strip using the new vocabulary words.

CONCLUSION

When students come into my chemistry classroom, they often have no prior knowledge of the vocabulary because they have never been exposed to it or they haven't internalized the terms introduced in previous classes. My goal is to help students comprehend the new terms to better understand concepts rather than merely memorize the words and their definitions. I believe students remember terms better with repeated exposure to meaningful contexts. After the experiment, students see their comprehension of the vocabulary words increase as they move across the columns in the worksheet. Using the new terms in a quickwrite also reinforces the students' understanding.

REFERENCES

Blachowicz, C., & Fisher, P. J. (2002). *Teaching vocabulary in all classrooms.* Upper Saddle River, NJ: Merrill/Prentice Hall.

The vocabulary worksheet was adapted from an activity created by Jane Rumulo, English and AVID teacher at Granite Hills High School, Porterville, CA.

Working with Meanings

Students need to manipulate words to deepen their understanding of the words' meanings. Marzano (2004) cites a number of studies that support the assumption that students require "repeated and varied exposure to words, during which they revise their initial understandings" (p. 73). This chapter provies multiple activities that promote such exposures. Schwanenflugel, Stahl, and McFalls (1997) explain that as students work with words over time, their comprehension of the word increases. Students begin to understand multiple meanings of the words as well as nuances and connotations in how the words are used.

Teachers understand that learning words through context is difficult; in fact there is little evidence to show that contextual clues alone give enough information for word acquisition (Marzano, 2004). However, when context is used in addition to other strategies, learning is enhanced. Eileen Boland, Cathy Cirimele, and Laurie Goodman ("Shades of Meaning: Relating and Expanding Word Knowledge") all present activities that include context clues within a larger activity to encourage students to create meaning.

Activities written by Mike Olenchalk, Joe Perez, Cathy Blanchfield, and Laurie Goodman ("Word Posters That Link Key Concepts") encourage students to learn content-area academic vocabulary. It is through relating concept vocabulary to other words that make these activities effective. Lehr, Osborn, and Hiebert (2004) suggest that students learn words by association with other words, especially words that they are already familiar with.

Karen Yelton-Curtis and Rebecca Wheeler both present activities that allow students to manipulate words to create a deeper understanding. Students deepen their understanding of meanings by working with connotations.

Through all of the activities in this chapter, students begin to understand words at what Baker, Simmons, and Kame'enui (1995) call the *comprehension* level. It is at this level students are able to understand multiple meanings and nuances of single words.

REFERENCES

Baker, S., Simmons, D., & Kame'enui, E. (1995). *Vocabulary acquisition: Synthesis of research.* Eugene, OR: National Center to Improve the Tools of Educators.

Lehr, F., Osborn, J., & Hiebert, E. H. (2004). A *focus on vocabulary.* Honolulu: Pacific Resources for Education and Learning.

Marzano, R. (2004). *Building background knowledge for academic achievement: Research on what works in schools.* Alexandria, VA: Association for Supervision and Curriculum Development.

Schwanenflugel, P. J., Stahl, S. A., & McFalls, E. L. (1997). *Partial word knowledge and vocabulary growth during reading comprehension* (Research Report No. 76). Athens, GA: National Reading Research Center.

WORD ASSOCIATIONS WITH LITERARY CHARACTERS

Karen Yelton-Curtis

One of my goals is to help students make connections within and beyond the English language arts curriculum. I have found that connections are critical to effective vocabulary instruction; students experience greater success with word learning when they are able to link new words to existing concepts, or to specific material that is the focus of study in class. Alvermann and Phelps (2002) emphasize that new words "can only be mastered through repeated experience within meaningful context" (p. 247).

Novels provide fertile ground for enriching students' vocabularies. Even though certain words should be introduced to students to improve their comprehension of a text, these are not necessarily the words that students will remember once they have finished reading. Students have shown me that new words associated with literary characters or aspects of plot are more likely to be recalled and used in their own writing.

Although teachers can create word banks from classroom texts, students should be given the opportunity to develop the word bank for the activity. Beck, McKeown, and Kucan (2002) recommend that teachers should consider:

- the importance and usefulness of the words. They should appear routinely across a variety of domains.
- the instructional potential of the words. Students should be able to associate the new words with other words and concepts.
- the level of conceptual comprehension. Students may understand a general concept and a new word crystallizes the concept.

Following these suggestions, I developed this word association activity during a unit on *The Adventures of Huckleberry Finn* (Twain, 2002). Students were engaged with the characters in the book and their interest presented an opportunity for enhanced vocabulary instruction.

PROCEDURE

I introduce the word association activity when my students are about halfway through the reading of the novel. When they enter class they see the word bank on the whiteboard: *adroit, audacious, autonomous, barbarous, bibliophile, credulous, devout, pragmatic, prevaricator, recalcitrant, scrupulous,* and *treacherous.* I begin class with a quickwrite that asks students to list characters they have encountered in the book and the qualities they associate with the characters. Students then share what they have written.

I tell students that the purpose of the activity is to help them expand their descriptive vocabulary. Then I sketch a four-column chart for students to copy in their class notebooks. A word from the word bank is written in column one, the definition and category of speech for the word is noted in column two, the name of a character from the novel is entered in column three, and corroborating evidence from the novel is written in column four. Students arm themselves with dictionaries and proceed to fill in the chart; the goal is to assign at least one character to each new word by the end of the period. Because I typically have had a half-class set of dictionaries, students work with a partner. Figure 18–1 is an example of a student-created chart.

One benefit of the activity is that students vary their word associations. The differences arise in end-of-class discussions or warm-up reviews in the following days. For example, in working with the word *adroit*—which means skillful and adept, especially in dangerous or difficult circumstances—students would likely associate the word with Huck in the instance of the elaborate staging of his own "murder"; however, students also have associated the word with Jim because of Jim's ability to avoid capture as a runaway slave.

The chart provides concrete references for learning new words. Follow-up activities can include student-to-student quizzes in which one student provides the word and a partner gives a definition and supporting text evidence; focused passage analysis in which students work directly with the text that supports their word association and describe how the character's thoughts or actions support the word definition; and an antonym game in which students cite characters who do not fit the definition of a word and provide text evidence for their choices. Students should be encouraged to incorporate their new vocabulary into essays they write about the literature. I tell students that I look for vocabulary words when I score their writing and highlight those that I find.

FIGURE 18–1
Example of a Student-Created Chart

Word	Definition	Finn character	Evidence from the novel
adroit	(adj.) skillful and adept, especially in dangerous or difficult circumstances	Huck	Huck shows that he is adroit when he fakes his murder to escape from Pap.
audacious	(adj.) taking or willing to take risks; unrestrained by convention	Huck	Huck puts his freedom on the line when he talks to Judith Loftus (the shanty woman).
autonomous	(adj.) independent, self-contained	Huck	Huck's knowledge of nature helps him survive on Jackson's Island and on the raft.
barbarous	(adj.) primitive in culture and customs; savage or brutal	Pap	Pap has a scruffy appearance and when he is drunk, beats Huck.
bibliophile	(n) a book lover or collector	Widow, Miss Watson	The widow promotes the Bible and Miss Watson teaches Huck from books.
credulous	(adj.) tending to believe too readily; gullible	Huck	Huck is credulous in the beginning when he believes Tom's lies about the gang.
devout	(adj.) deeply religious; earnest, sincere	Jim	Jim is devout when he tells Huck how much he appreciates him for fooling the slave catchers.

CONCLUSION

I enjoy delving into a thesaurus to prepare a word bank for my students, who are quite pleased with their abilities to connect new words to their prior knowledge about the characters in *The Adventures of Huckleberry Finn*. Students also enjoy working with a partner because it allows them to negotiate the wording of the supporting evidence from the novel. Alvermann and Phelps (2002) value discussion in vocabulary study, saying that it is important for students to use their own language to explain new words. The result is a more thorough processing of the words' meanings.

Students appreciate vocabulary study if they can see uses for new words beyond classroom-based reading and writing. With adolescents so absorbed in personalities promoted online and through traditional media, and looking for ways to accurately describe them as writing skills mature, the middle school and high school grades are ripe with opportunity to teach vocabulary.

REFERENCES

Alvermann, D. E., & Phelps, S. F. (2002). *Content reading and literacy: Succeeding in today's diverse classrooms*. Boston: Allyn & Bacon.

Beck, I. L., McKeown, M. G., & Kucan, L. (2002). *Bringing words to life: Robust vocabulary instruction*. New York: Guilford Press.

Graff, G., & Phelan, J. (Eds.). (1995). *Adventures of Huckleberry Finn: A Case Study in Critical Controversy*. New York: Bedford Books.

Twain, Mark. (2002). *The Adventures of Huckleberry Finn*. New York: Barnes and Noble.

KEY WORD COLLECTION: A NEW WAY TO FOCUS ON MULTIPLE MEANINGS OF WORDS

Eileen Boland

"Guess what?" An enthusiastic hand shoots up. It begins to wave as if it were a pendulum.

"What is it, Natalie?" I ask curiously. This student is normally very quiet in class.

"Last night on a TV special, I saw an inaugural party for President Bush. And inaugural *is one of my words that I found in my biography of Franklin Roosevelt."*

Wanting to know more about what she saw, I question her further. "What exactly did you see at the inaugural party?"

"I saw people wearing expensive clothes who were dancing to some music a band was playing. President Bush looked jaunty in the video just like President Roosevelt did at his inaugural."

"How did you know about President Roosevelt?"

"It's in my biography I'm reading on Roosevelt. I wrote jaunty *down too," Natalie replied.*

Being proud of her observations, I comment, "Way to go! Keep on looking for your words and using them whenever you can."

Natalie is becoming a word collector. She not only recognizes the use of a word, but also integrates new words into her vocabulary as she speaks. This is what learning vocabulary is all about.

PROCEDURE

Opportunity for vocabulary growth is important. Although reading provides a plethora of words, students need to work with these words in a number of ways in order to integrate the meanings into their knowledge base. Context alone is an insufficient way of learning new words. Baumann and Kame'enui (1991) state that students need a definitional approach in addition to learning words in context while reading; the key word collection paper is one approach that has proven effective in my classroom.

As Natalie reads, she writes down an important word from the book that she does not know in the left column of the collection form. She then looks up the word in the dictionary and writes all the possible definitions in the center column. A copy of her word-collection form is shown in Figure 19–1. Turning back to the reading, she rereads the sentence that contains the new word. Based on the context of the biography, Natalie puts a check mark next to the definition that applies to how the word was used in the sentence. Then, she writes its etymology or word history in the right column.

Federal Biographical Institute's Key word collection for:

Franklin Roosevelt

Learning new words is very important as you proceed through your readings. By learning these words based on the context of the sentence/paragraph along with the help of a dictionary, you can greatly increase your vocabulary knowledge as an agent of the FBI.

DIRECTIONS: Write down a minimum of 15 new words. Write the word as you come across it in your reading. Then, get a dictionary and write down the first three definitions. Put a check mark next to the definition that applies to your reading. In the last box, give its word history.

New Word	Possible definitions. Put a check mark next to the definition that applies.	Word History
inaugural	1. of, for, or having to do with an inauguration ✓ 2. beginning; first 3. the address or speech made by a person when formally admitted to office	
jaunty	1. easy and lively; sprightly; carefree ✓ 2. smart and stylish	<middle french gentil noble gentle<Latin gentilis
prominent	✓ 1. well known or important 2. that catches the eye; easy to see 3. standing out; projecting	<Latin prominentum

FIGURE 19–1 Student Key Word Collection

Natalie went on to collect many more words. I recommend that the teacher set a minimum number of words—around 15 words—to be collected. In this way, the students know what is expected.

EXTENSIONS

Multiple opportunities for learning these new words must occur. For example, students can construct word posters combining 10 of the most important words from the text, including the etymologies and definitions that fit best with the context for each. Journal writing, story charts, concept ladders, and open minds are just a few examples of the many activities that incorporate writing. Personal word dictionaries and individual word walls may also be made.

Through many exposures to these words, Natalie will soon "own" them. They will become part of the 3,000 new words she learns during the year. By collecting key words, Natalie is well on her way into her adventure with words.

CONCLUSION

As a class, we discuss other words that students have noticed outside their reading. They refer to their key word collection paper as they check their words. Hands go up with examples to share. The enthusiasm is boundless, and learning new words becomes fun.

REFERENCE

Baumann, J. F., & Kame'enui, E. J. (1991). Research on vocabulary instruction: Ode to Voltaire. In J. Flood, J. M. Jensen, D. Lapp, & J. R. Squire (Eds.), *Handbook on teaching the English language arts* (pp. 604–632). New York: Macmillan.

WORD POSTERS THAT LINK KEY CONCEPTS

Laurie Goodman

The floodgates have opened more than once during a literature focus unit or a content-area unit. My students have seen tears in my eyes, and I have handed tissues to them as well—tears of joy and tears of sorrow from mental movies of the unspeakable events that have occurred during the history of our world. Some students sit bewildered and ask, "How can you see the events from these words on this page?" They are in the process of developing the ability to visualize the passages that they are reading.

I am fortunate to have students who love to draw, and many of my good artists are the same students who talk about words becoming images in their minds. Visualization is a comprehension strategy, and I extend this strategy to our vocabulary words. My goal is for students to acquire an in-depth understanding of the vocabulary words that they encounter as they read. Word posters that link related words to a concept increase my students' concept knowledge.

BREAK OUT THE DRAWING PAPER

My students respond to the assignment of creating word posters from our vocabulary words in a variety of ways. Some students are elated to have an art component; others dread the assignment because of their lack of artistic ability. I remind them that they will not be graded on their artistic ability. The requirements for the assignment include the following:

1. Choose two words from the unit's word wall.
2. Brainstorm a visual representation of each word on scratch paper.
3. Draft a paragraph explaining each illustration.
4. Conference with two group members to revise paragraphs.
5. Conference with the teacher to edit the work.
6. Create a final word poster presenting the vocabulary word, a paragraph using the word, and the illustration.

LINKING THE WORDS

My students make word posters after we have spent some time studying the content of the unit. Students are moving to the in-depth concept knowledge level, and word posters allow them to show their understanding of the key words and the word

FIGURE 20–1 Students'
Linked Word Posters

phrases of a unit. I can see their level of understanding as they extend the words to other words that are related to a key concept. Linking the word posters together to show integration of several words as they relate to a key concept is the method we use as a class to further our knowledge level (see Figure 20–1). Students examine the word posters after they present them to the class and look for relationships between them. They will either identify a key term from the word wall or decide on a concept that fits the related posters.

For example, Chris illustrated the word *Quakers*, Jenny illustrated *prejudice*, Ben illustrated *Underground Railroad*, Frank illustrated *equality*, and Beth illustrated the name *John Brown*; these are all words that are part of our unit on slavery. As students evaluate the posters and hear the explanations read aloud, their knowledge level increases. Students discuss in their groups the associations these words have with each other and link the words to the key concept, *abolitionism*.

Students link their posters by actually attaching them to each other—they tape or glue each poster to another at the top margin. Then students write the key concept in big red letters on a sentence strip and post it on a bulletin board above

FIGURE 20–2 A Student's Quickwrite

> **Abolitionism**
>
> Both the Quakers and the people who developed and maintained the Underground Railroad wanted equality for all Americans. These two groups of people did not believe in Slavery and risked their own freedom to ensure that slaves would be free once they made it Canada.
>
> An important aspect of these two groups is that they used non-violent means to fight against slavery and for equality. I believe the Quakers and the people who maintained the system of escape through the Underground Railroad set up a model for other non-violent leaders like Martin Luther King, Jr. to follow. They will continue to be an example of people that strive for equality and made a difference in the lives of others.

their linked word posters. There will be several groups of linked word posters on the bulletin board; each set has a different key word. This visual display of vocabulary words that relate to a key concept is a powerful learning tool for students.

QUICKWRITE TO SHOW KNOWLEDGE

When our word posters are up, I list the key concepts that students have chosen on the chalkboard and ask them to pick three key concepts and write about them. These quickwrites show me and the students their level of concept knowledge. Figure 20–2 is an example of a student quickwrite on abolitionism.

CONCLUSION

Students usually are able to write about each concept without turning around to check the wall, and they should be able to include the linked vocabulary words in their quickwrites. I am amazed at the level of understanding this activity produces for students.

21

VOCABULARY DEVELOPMENT IN THE SCIENCE CLASSROOM

Michael Olenchalk

Traditional vocabulary instruction in the science classroom has focused on word recognition rather than on understanding terms and concepts. Many of the vocabulary lessons that are offered in the back of textbooks ask students to use essential terms in a sentence. Ancillary materials in teacher resource packages include crossword puzzles and fill-in-the-blank questioning strategies. Although these activities increase student exposure to the terms, they do little to promote comprehension of the subject matter. Vocabulary instruction that is not directly linked to student comprehension will not allow students to explain the term or concept, connect new information with prior knowledge, or apply this knowledge in the future.

Often, students in the science classroom encounter terms such as *nucleotides* and *guanine* that might not be part of their working vocabulary. In fact, they may not have even heard the words before. If a new term has never been encountered, students cannot connect it with prior knowledge. Prior knowledge or previous experience provides a scaffold for new information. All sensory information is processed and categorized based on relationships. These relationships can be cognitive or kinesthetic. New information is placed on what might be termed the most appropriate location in the brain based on these relationships. When I design a vocabulary activity, I assume that the students will have had no experience with the information. With this in mind, I designed an activity that will build background knowledge.

PROCEDURE

The beginning of the lesson on DNA involves an activity. I begin every chapter with a prereading activity to establish background information or prior knowledge. The prereading activity is sensory in that it is something the students are familiar with and kinesthetic from the standpoint of students manipulating materials. This is followed by a reading activity.

The steps in the prereading activity include the following:

1. Arrange students into groups of four.
2. Give each group of students a puzzle to put together.
3. Upon completion of the puzzle, ask the students to respond to the following prompts: What can you tell me about how puzzles are put together? What type of processes did you engage in to complete the puzzle?
4. Allow the students to share their responses at their tables.

5. Allow students to engage in a whole-class discussion based on their responses.
6. Discuss the relationship between the puzzle (how things fit together) and the arrangement of the DNA or RNA molecule.

The steps in the reading activity are:

1. Assign each group of students a section in the textbook to read together.
2. Have students decide what the main idea or concept is as they read. They may use section headings, bold font terms, and italicized words as clues. They record their ideas on a piece of binder paper.
3. On that same piece of paper, have students each make a T-chart; the left side of the chart will consist of science terms they are familiar with, and the right side will consist of terms they are unfamiliar with.
4. Have the students compare concepts and their charts.
5. Each table is responsible for developing a vocabulary chart.

Figure 21–1 is an example of a T-chart for the structure of DNA concept that my students developed as they read.

The chart that each group develops will list those terms that relate to specific sections in the textbook. They may include familiar and unfamiliar terms. Each group will select the terms that they perceive to be crucial in understanding the concept or main idea. The answers might vary from year to year. It is up to the instructor to make sure that each key term is addressed. Once the vocabulary group has been established, the students will brainstorm ideas about the message the author is trying to convey; is it a process, procedure, protocol, or explanation of terms? Through the reading context and discussion, they begin to understand the meaning of the words. The groups will then quickwrite a brief paragraph that employs the familiar and unfamiliar terms and attempts to clarify the concept. As the students read, clarify, discuss, and write their understanding of the words grows.

Compare these two paragraphs about the structure of DNA:

DNA is made up of four nitrogen bases: adenine, thymine, guanine, and cytosine. A nucleotide contains a nitrogen base, a phosphate group, and a special sugar called deoxyribose. The nucleotides fit together like puzzle pieces. They follow certain pairing rules, which means that they can fit together only one way, just like the pieces of a puzzle. Adenine will pair only with thymine while cytosine will pair only with guanine. Thousands of nucleotides connected to one another make up a strand of DNA. DNA is able to copy itself; this process is called replication. The term *replication* is similar in meaning to the word *duplicate*.

Cytosine, guanine, thymine, and adenine are nitrogen bases. A nucleotide is made up of phosphates, nitrogen bases, and dexoyribose. The process of DNA making an exact copy of itself is called replication.

Familiar Science Terms	Unfamiliar Science Terms
duplicate	nucleotides
sugar	adenine
base	guanine
pairing	cytosine
copy	thymine
	replication
	dexyribose

FIGURE 21–1 Sample T-Chart of DNA Concept

The first paragraph clearly demonstrates a higher level of understanding. The writing is connected to the prereading activity. The first paragraph gives specific information about the structure of DNA and attempts to define how things work together. The second paragraph is simply a series of sentences that may have been taken directly from a textbook. In essence, the terms have been repeated, and although the sentences provide information in context, it is difficult to determine if the student comprehends the topic.

I prefer to have the students write paragraphs before extending the activity into flip charts or word sorting activities. The most important portion of the lesson is to make sure that the appropriate terms have been selected to best describe the concept to be learned.

EXTENSION ACTIVITIES

Two extension activities that I use with my science students to further enhance understanding are flip charts and word sorts.

Flip Charts

Each student at the table can develop a flip chart that addresses the concept and the related vocabulary terms (Tompkins, 2004). The flip chart consists of half sheets of paper, each containing a sentence or two pertaining to the concept, stapled at the top for easy "flipping." Figure 21–2 is an example of four pages from a student flip chart.

FIGURE 21–2 Sample Pages from a Student Flip Chart

> DNA is made of <u>nucleotides</u>. <u>Nucleotides</u> fit together like pieces of a puzzle. Puzzles can only fit together in certain ways. Nucleotides are made up of different parts.
>
> Card 1

> <u>Nucleotides</u> are made with four <u>nitrogen bases</u>. These bases are <u>adenine</u>, <u>thymine</u>, <u>guanine</u> and <u>cytosine</u>. Each nucleotide contains only one <u>nitrogen base</u>. <u>Nucleotides</u> (all) contain a <u>phosphate group</u> and a <u>sugar</u> called <u>deoxyribose</u>.
>
> Card 2

> So each <u>nucleotide</u> contains one <u>nitrogen base</u>, one <u>sugar</u>, and one <u>phosphate group</u>. <u>Nucleotides</u> can join together. This is called <u>base pairing</u>. Each <u>nucleotide</u> can only <u>base pair</u> with its partner: <u>adenine with thymine</u> and <u>guanine with cytosine</u>.
>
> Card 3

> Since <u>nucleotides</u> can only <u>base pair</u> one way, we say they fit like a puzzle. Puzzles only fit together one way. DNA is made up of thousands of <u>nucleotides</u> linked together make a <u>strand</u>.
>
> Card 4

The table group will decide how the term is used in the text and what it is trying to explain. One chart stays at the table and the other charts will be distributed to other tables. Each table will exchange charts, ensuring that the whole text has been covered. These charts can be used for review activities and are stored in shoe boxes at each table. In effect, the textbook content and related vocabulary have been jigsawed.

Word Sorts

Concepts are written on large index "concept" cards and distributed at each table. Students then identify specific vocabulary terms that relate to the concept and write them on 3 × 5-inch cards. The large index cards as well as the 3 × 5-inch "vocabulary" cards are then posted (Tompkins, 2004). When teachers develop the concepts, it is considered a closed sort; when students develop the concepts, it is considered an open sort.

CONCLUSION

Students must be able to internalize, synthesize, and apply the information that is encountered in the text. To do this, students must be immersed in both content and context. Students must understand that certain vocabulary words are related to specific concepts and to fully comprehend the concept, they must first seek the meaning of the related words. Students who can use a term in an appropriate context demonstrate the first level of understanding. When they can connect new vocabulary with previous knowledge, use the vocabulary in a purposeful manner to explain a concept, and apply this new knowledge to future learning, they have developed an in-depth understanding of both the vocabulary and the concept.

REFERENCE

Tompkins, G. (2004). *Teaching writing: Balancing process and product.* Upper Saddle River, NJ: Merrill/Prentice Hall.

22

SENSITIZING STUDENTS TO SHADES OF MEANING: THE SYNONYM CONTINUUM

Rebecca Wheeler

When my students write their end-of-year portfolio reflection essays, most of them write that they had little experience with poetry analysis before the class. We work with poetry all year, and because of the condensed language of poetry, it is the genre that most requires us to focus on individual words. Near the beginning of the year, as part of our word study in poetry, we do lessons on denotation and connotation. We brainstorm synonyms for *woman* and *man*, and students have fun classifying those with positive connotations and those with more derogatory ones. We turn to a word such as *thin* and generate synonyms, and then students try to decide particular denotative as well as connotative meanings of the synonyms. At some point during one of these activities, I noticed that students often had to turn to a dictionary to look up several words (while doing *thin*, for example, most of them didn't know the word *svelte*), and I saw valuable group discussions about shades of meaning. I decided I wanted my students thinking about words in this way all the time, so I started asking them to do a regular vocabulary assignment I call the *synonym continuum*.

PROCEDURE

When I studied for my credential, the textbook for my methods class contained an assignment called a *character continuum*. In this assignment, students map out characters from a work, often along a line of extremes but sometimes in another graphic map that shows relationships. For example, while studying *Macbeth*, a group of students might produce a character continuum like this:

    witches   Duncan   Lady Macbeth   Macbeth   Banquo

The students then explain what their continuum represents; in this example, it might represent who the students believe has the most power at the beginning of the play (students might argue that the witches are controlling people's destinies, that Duncan is the ruler of the land and has just executed the Thane of Cawdor, that Lady Macbeth is strong and influential, that Macbeth is a high-ranking official, etc., so the continuum moves from most powerful to least powerful). Of course, the way the characters are mapped out depends on the group making the map, not only for interpreting the characters but also for deciding on which criteria their map is based. The *Macbeth* example uses power as the criterion, but other groups might rank characters according to their social status or their personal integrity. I found this assignment to be a good way to get students talking about characters and about fine distinctions among them; the synonym continuum assignment, an adaptation of the assignment that uses words instead of characters, is a good way to get students talking about words and the fine distinctions among them.

A synonym continuum works much the same way as a character continuum, except that the focus is on a group of synonyms. Perhaps students are learning the word *designate*. If they look it up in a thesaurus, they find synonyms such as *indicate, name, specify, pinpoint, select, appoint, choose, nominate, assign,* and *identify*. Students must map out these synonyms along a continuum (if the thesaurus entry contains many synonyms, like this example, students don't need to use all of them; four or five is a good number). A continuum for this word, based on only some of the synonyms found in the thesaurus, might look like this:

> nominate　　　choose　　　select　　　pinpoint　　　designate　　　assign

This continuum represents movement from weaker, less commanding synonyms for *designate* to synonyms that seem to imply less freedom of choice—*assign*. Often, I ask my students to try to supply additional words (not found in the thesaurus) for one or both ends of the continuum; in this example, students might add *suggest* to the left end of the continuum or *command* to the right end.

Once students have placed the words along a continuum, they must explain what the continuum itself represents. In the preceding example, it represents something like *weaker* to *stronger* words; many continuums represent negative to positive connotations. Students are not always restricted to mapping along a single line. Sometimes students want to show that two or three synonyms are very closely related, so they cluster those together; then the vocabulary word is in the center, and another synonym or two are clustered in another corner. As long as the students can explain why they have mapped out the words as they did, I'm happy. The point is to think about the vocabulary word in relation to other words. Sometimes, the students learn some additional words along the way because they must find out the definition of a synonym before they can map it; but always, this activity forces them to *place* a word's definition much more specifically than most vocabulary activities that simply find creative ways to get students to memorize definitions.

VARIATIONS

This activity can easily be customized for the needs of a particular lesson. When students are just learning to create continuums, teachers might have five or six volunteers hold up cards with a synonym on each card, and then the entire class could arrange those students in a lineup. The activity works very well in small groups because students must discuss different options for arranging the words. This can be extended into writing activities as well as interpretive activities. For example, a teacher might use this to encourage students to use a greater variety of active verbs—a continuum of synonyms for *walk*, perhaps. Most of the time, students in my class developed personal vocabulary lists and made vocabulary cards, and the synonym continuum was one part of their vocabulary card on each word. (This activity doesn't work very well for every word; some very specific nouns, for example, don't have a handy list of synonyms in the thesaurus. Students had alternate vocabulary activities if this was the case.)

The synonym continuum was very effective for sensitizing my students to shades of meaning. When students studied poems, for example, and ran across a word they needed to look up, they were less likely to substitute the first synonym in the dictionary; instead, they often discussed precisely what the particular word might mean. They learned to ask questions such as, "If *svelte* means *thin*, why didn't the poet just use *thin*? How is *svelte* different from *thin*?" (Okay, I never heard that exact line, but I really did hear my students saying similar things about words.)

CONCLUSION

Many of the juniors I teach will go on to take Advanced Placement English, and, partly because of this activity, they are ready to intelligently discuss the effects of a particular word in a piece. Questions on the SAT verbal section, especially the analogies and sentence completions, provide more than one answer that appears to be correct, and a student's ability to choose which answer is *most* correct depends on his or her ability to distinguish subtle differences in meaning. Students who are sensitized to shades of meaning should be more likely to look carefully through their options rather than blindly choosing the first synonym they see.

Most important, however, asking students to relate a word to other words gives students a mental "home" for the word. Students are able to relate the new word to words they already know. This is a skill that crosses every grade level; it is not just high school students who will benefit from this activity. I've often heard people describe the brain as a set of file cabinets. If our files are organized, the analogy goes, we can find something later; it's easier to find something if it's linked to something else we know that's related. If we help students link new words to existing "files" of words in their brains, these new words are more likely to be neatly filed with related words in their brain and thus be accessible later.

23

CONNOTATIONS: ECLECTIC AND ELECTRIC

Joe Perez

Students in my class are taught early in the school year that *denotation* is the precise dictionary definition. *Connotation*, on the other hand, is the emotional and experiential meaning of a word; the way a word sometimes makes your heart race with joy or sink with sadness. For example, the word *war* can bring different powerful responses depending on one's life as a soldier, refugee, or antiwar advocate. Connotations, then, are eclectic and often electric with intensity—varying according to the individual. Connotations, I tell my students, are bristling with possibilities and sometimes controversy. For a long time, I have had a poster-sized Kipling quote on my classroom wall: "Words are, of course, the most powerful drugs in the world." This gets to the heart of connotation.

READ WITH CARE

Readers must tread carefully through what they read because connotations are everywhere. To appreciate connotations, it would be helpful to know words such as *empathy, irony,* and *hyperbole. Empathy* urges the readers to "get into the skin" of someone, as Tennessee Williams said, even though it may be futile or at least difficult. The proper noun *Auschwitz* can be objectively defined in its World War II context, but to spend time there in your mind, walking through the dungeons of death, thinking of *Schindler's List* or Anne Frank's life, can give the readers insight and the glimmering of the horror. *Irony* certainly is relevant for a connotative understanding of *peace treaty*, for instance, as it relates to 19th-century American government policy toward indigenous people or present-day Northern Ireland. *Hyperbole* comes into play with words such as *politician* and *lawyer*. Cynical readers may immediately think of a political cartoon of a stereotypical, avaricious Washingtonian raking in taxpayers' money for his own benefit.

MICROCONNOTATIONS

Young readers who can be sensitive to connotations will begin to appreciate the subtleties of language, not only in big contexts of plot or theme but also in syntax. Every word is there for a reason, especially as one reads more concentrated writing, such as a short story or poetry. When Christopher Marlowe beseeches his sweetheart to "come with me and be my *love*," what does the word *love* connote? How is it different when compared with John Donne's saying as he reluctantly leaves his wife for a time, "But we by a *love* so much refined / that we not know what it is." What is Donne's connotation of *love*? Has the reader experienced both connotations of *love*?

CONNOTATIONS AND CONTROVERSIES: SOME ACTIVITIES

I teach connotations through the reading of fiction, expository selections, and primary sources. I choose a variety of texts concerning the same subject and a few key concepts. As we read through each source, I stop whenever we come to one of the key concepts to discuss the connotation of that word in context. I model the type of questions I want students to ask:

- What does the author mean when he or she uses the key concept in this sentence?
- Is he or she trying to evoke a certain attitude in the reader through the use of this word?
- How does the meaning here compare to past experiences you have had with this word?

Before long, the students are stopping on their own and asking similar questions of each other. In this way, they begin to appreciate the power of connotation.

Connotations in a real-world situation hit home to me in a 5-week institute on early slave cultures in the American colonies. Several scholarly speakers referred to slaves transported to Americans as *immigrants*. They did this as a method of statistically calculating all newcomers in the 17th century. Several of my colleagues took offense to the word *immigrant*; the connotation of that word was "too polite," too inaccurate to characterize the forcible and deadly sea journey.

The scholarly presenters dealing with dry statistics did not at first see the controversy in not using the emotionally loaded word *slave* and how *immigrant*, although accurate in a denotative way, was not acceptable to many in the group. In the days that followed, the word *reparation* was used to ask other speakers if descendants of slaves should be given compensation for their ancestors' forced labor and travail. This word, too, was connotatively full of emotion and grief for many in my group.

Just recently, the California legislature voted unanimously to ask the federal government to formulate a plan of *reparation* for slave descendants. It would be a good class assignment for students to note how this word is used in relation to the historical event. Certainly controversy will be rife. Although many will see the issue objectively from a denotative, dollar-and-cents viewpoint, for others, the connotative meaning will be compelling. Will students themselves care about and develop opinions about this issue? Can they empathize?

George Orwell was a writer keenly aware of connotations. In *Animal Farm* (1946), for instance, the idea of equality has many controversial applications, depending on circumstances. In the short story "Shooting an Elephant" in my *Elements of Literature* (1997) textbook, Orwell must deal with the concept of empire building, the concept of British control over large populations. Orwell was caught up in what critic James Harrison, in *Elements of Literature*, called "a search for equilibrium" between native cultural practices and "Anglocentric" behaviors forced on these native populations because it would "civilize" them. Orwell was caught between his own "hatred of the empire" and the fact that, as he states at the beginning of his story, he was "hated by large numbers of people—the only time in my life I have been important enough for this to happen to me." To Orwell, the word *empire* connoted repugnant feelings based on a negative experience.

Another good exercise for students is to discuss the word *empire* after reading the story, finding its denotation and then applying the emotional and experiential concepts. Again we could use concepts such as *empathy, irony,* and *hyperbole* to think about the word. For instance, can a student relate to Orwell's connotation of *empire* that would include exploitation, futility, and cruelty? Perhaps this would be a good place to bring in U.S. history and specifically the Declaration of Independence—Americans as victims of empire. Or students might consider if we have our own empire building going on. If so, in what ways? How do you (the student) feel about that?

CONCLUSION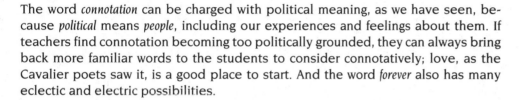

The word *connotation* can be charged with political meaning, as we have seen, because *political* means *people*, including our experiences and feelings about them. If teachers find connotation becoming too politically grounded, they can always bring back more familiar words to the students to consider connotatively; love, as the Cavalier poets saw it, is a good place to start. And the word *forever* also has many eclectic and electric possibilities.

REFERENCES

Elements of literature. (1997). New York: Holt, Reinhart and Winston.
Orwell, G. (1946). *Animal farm.* New York: Harper & Row.

24

VENERABLE TEACHING

Cathy Cirimele

Teaching juniors is exciting, but teaching them *The Scarlet Letter* (Hawthorne, 1980) can be a torturous experience for all of us. Probably the biggest challenge at the beginning of the novel is the vocabulary. Hawthorne's word choice is sophisticated and complex; but in addition to that, many of the most important words in the text are used in multiple ways. Nuances in meaning, that only the best readers can understand, are created.

Each time I teach the novel, I seek ways to make it more accessible to my students. For example, I have left out "The Custom House" chapter and taught it in the middle, end, and beginning of the book. This chapter is probably the most difficult for students because it only vaguely touches on the love affair of Hester Prynne and Arthur Dimmesdale. Once students begin these characters' part of the story, they often become hooked and the diction and syntax become less foreboding. However, the only proper time to have them read "The Custom House" chapter is before they get into the story of Hester and Dimmesdale. Not only does Hawthorne make some important comments about his life as a writer, but he sets the tone and thematic ideas here. It needs to be read. So, what is the problem? First of all, the syntax and diction are so sophisticated that some students claim that they are not even reading English—the same thing they say when they read Shakespeare. Also, most of the important vocabulary words, many of which show up on the PSAT and SAT tests, have multiple meanings. My task is to always help students not only understand what the words mean on a literal, denotative level, but also access the connotations and the various contextual ways in which Hawthorne uses them in the text.

What have I done to help them? Some of my most successful vocabulary lessons for *The Scarlet Letter* have revolved around word walls and word posters. As we begin "The Custom House," I put the difficult words that students need help with on butcher paper at the front of the class. We discuss the meaning of each word as it is used in the context of the passage. This word wall stays up as we read the novel. We refer to it whenever we recognize a word or see a different way in which it is used in the text. A further activity is to assign each student a word to use in a word poster, on which they write the word, a definition of the word, an illustration, and a sentence using the word. These can also be posted around the classroom and used as references to the text. Other activities might include flip books, word chains, and vocabulary cards. Because some of these words can be used in a variety of ways, students need to work with the most important words and their different meanings as they appear in the text.

A good example of this is the word *venerable*, which usually means *honored* or *respected*. Hawthorne uses this word so frequently that by the time students are nearly finished with the book, they chuckle every time it appears. It seems to be

Hawthorne's favorite word. Another word he uses frequently in the text is *ignominious*, which often is used to mean *dishonorable*. Certainly Hawthorne uses other words frequently, so what is so special about his use of these two words? They are at the core of the major thematic ideas of the novel. Hawthorne uses these two words interchangeably with such diverse characters as Hester, Dimmesdale, Chillingworth, and others in the text. This is very confusing for students. They believe that once they learn one meaning for a word, that is the only way the word will be used. Hawthorne, however, had other ideas: He twisted these two words and used them ironically, satirically, sarcastically, and sometimes in opposition to what they usually mean. Does this frustrate students? Yes, it does. My job as their teacher is to moderate that level of frustration so that it does not capsize them or stop them from reading the novel. I need to find a way to show them that the meaning of these words is dependent on the context in which they are used.

PROCEDURE

One way to do this is through a technique called semantic word maps (California Department of Education, 2000). This strategy gives students a way to keep track of the different uses of vocabulary in the text and in particular these two words (see Figures 24–1 and 24–2). The most common definition of the word is cited along with the other definitions that are applicable. Students develop a cluster in which they place the word to be studied in the central hub of the web; students may choose a square, a rectangle, a circle, or any other form that intrigues them. One link from the hub then becomes a listing of the definitions of the word. As students find the vocabulary word in the text, they determine the meaning based on the context and then document to whom or to what it refers; thus the categories of character and definition become part of the cluster. Perhaps an additional part of the cluster could be a part of the quote in which the word appears.

This is an exercise that requires critical thinking. It can be done as a class with the teacher or a student writing the information on a piece of butcher paper or an overhead transparency. Just as effective is to allow students to make their own maps or clusters in small groups or individually and then compare them by sharing them

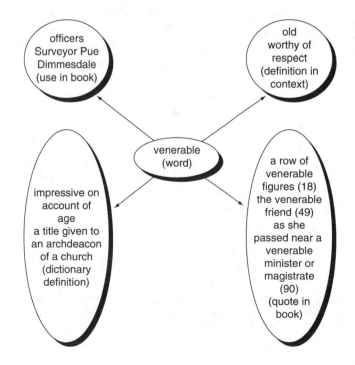

FIGURE 24–1 Student Vocabulary Map for *Venerable*

FIGURE 24–2 Student Vocabulary Map for *Ignominious*

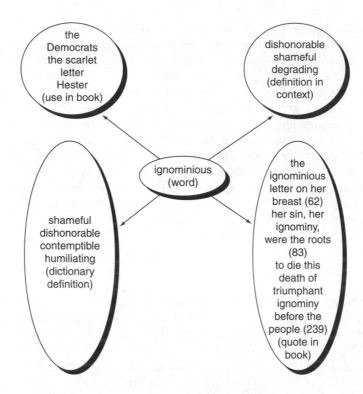

as a class. This strategy can be expanded past "The Custom House" and earlier chapters of the novel by having students keep track of the different ways the word is used throughout the novel. They can add a new cluster for each time the word is used in a new context, or they can create a whole new web each time. Either way, students engage in discussion about how Hawthorne uses one word to create new connotations throughout the book.

CONCLUSION

Working on this kind of vocabulary assignment not only reveals the complexity of language, but also enables students to access some of the subtler uses of words. It becomes a kind of game when the word is clustered and students can search for the meaning of the word in context. Like all great literature, *The Scarlet Letter* is a novel that asks more questions than it answers. If students can see that ambiguity is an important part of the novel, then they are able to understand that making questions is as important as answering them.

The ultimate use of this exercise is to expand it into an essay question. Certainly the most important discussions in the novel are sin, evil, and honor: Who is the sinner? Who should be honored? Who is evil? By looking deeper into Hawthorne's use of just two words in the novel, questions for an essay can be turned into thesis statements that explore some of the most important issues in this novel and in most great literature.

REFERENCES

California Department of Education. (2000). *Strategic teaching and learning: Standards-based instruction to promote content literacy in grades four through twelve.* Sacramento: California Department of Education.

Hawthorne, N. (1980). *The Scarlet letter.* Chicago: Signet.

25

SHADES OF MEANING: RELATING AND EXPANDING WORD KNOWLEDGE

Laurie Goodman

"But I really can provide a definition and an example for the word waste,
*Mrs. Goodman," Ali exclaimed. I refocused her to the slavery unit of study that we were
engaged in and asked her to relate the word to the unit. Ali is aware that words have
more than one meaning, but she is not always able to relate what she already knows
about the meaning of a word to the unit of study. I remind her that words can have very
different definitions, as well as definitions that are similar but that change according to
the context in which the word is being used.*

I watch Ali's face in deep thought as she tries to expand her knowledge of the word
waste *to encompass its usage in the current context. "OK, Mrs. Goodman. You're
right, my definition does not fit perfectly," Ali admits.*

SHADES OF MEANING

Ali needs to understand that words have shades of meaning. She can learn this
through a hands-on activity using shades of color and comparing these shades of
color to shades of meaning. We use color chips from a paint store to illustrate
shades of meaning.

With different color chips in hand, I point out that words have shades of meaning. I first choose the blue chip, which has six shades of color; each shade is different, but they all still represent the color blue. Next, I lay the red chip beside the
blue to show the contrast, and I ask the students to tell me the difference in the two
chips. Students think this is an easy task until they try to verbalize the difference in
detail. They find that by giving examples, they are able to illustrate the difference
in the two colors.

I am able to see that students are starting to make the connections with
shades of color and shades of meaning. Before we can carry this understanding to
our unit of study, we create a visual representation to remind us of what we have
learned. The students pick out their favorite color and a contrasting color and cut
their favorite color chip into pieces and cut one section from their contrasting color
chip. Next, they glue each piece in the top left corner of a 3 × 5-inch lined note card.
Before students can write on their cards, they create a rough draft describing the
color and giving an example, using complete sentences. Their last card has no color
pieces on its corner; it is the card that is used to describe how a single color has
varying shades as well as a contrasting color. This is the student's reflection card
to show understanding of the activity. After they have taken their drafts through the
writing process, they write the final copy on the note cards. Students' finished

FIGURE 25–1 A Student's Color Cards

> Ocean Blue
>
> My favorite shade of blue is between light blue and dark blue, and it has a green tint to it also. This shade of blue is the same color as the ocean at Morro Bay. It is also the paint color I chose for my room. It makes me feel calm and relaxed.

> Lollipop pink
>
> The color I chose in contrast to my favorite shade of blue is a middle shade of pink. This shade of pink is neither bright or soft. It can sometimes be seen in the flowers of a garden. It is a color that reminds me of childhood and immature things.

> Reflection
> From this activity I learned that there are many shades to a color and each shade can relate to each other. The shades of color were hard to describe and identify differently. Having a contrasting color to describe made it easier to describe my color. I have found this to be true with the definitions of words also, some relate to each other and some definitions are very different.

products are put on rings and shared with other students. Figure 25–1 is a sample of a completed set of cards.

TRANSFERRING OUR KNOWLEDGE

During the activity on shades of color, we discussed how words have shades of meaning. Now my students need to examine the dictionary and see that words can have shades of meaning. I put page 1472 from the *Random House Webster's College Dictionary* (1999) on the overhead. This page contains the words: *waste*, *watch*, and *water*. Next, I ask students to determine the number of definitions for each word, identify their parts of speech, and evaluate the definitions for the shades of meaning the words exhibit. They are very surprised to find out that *waste* has 30 meanings, *watch* has 22, and *water* has 37.

All three of these words relate to our unit on slavery. By using the dictionary and identifying shades of meaning, the students are able to recognize the difference in definitions. They realize that to be precise, they must use a dictionary to define a word that is part of their unit of study, but that the dictionary may not completely provide the level of understanding needed to explain the importance of the word to the unit.

As students reach full concept knowledge of a word, they will be able to relate the multiple shades of meaning it has to the unit of study. This performance activity requires the students to use multiple definitions in a dictionary and to fully elaborate on the connections between the definitions and the concept word. I require my students to use three or four definitions and to demonstrate knowledge of a multiple-meaning vocabulary word as it relates to a concept. In the example in Figure 25–2, an eighth-grade honors student has copied several definitions from the dictionary for the word *waste*. She chose seven definitions that were verbs and one definition that was a noun. Using the writing process, she applied her knowledge of slavery from the unit and related the definitions to the concept to slavery. After she finished integrating the definitions of the word *waste* as they relate to slavery, this

FIGURE 25–2 Student Writing Sample

Concept Word: Waste

Dictionary Definitions: 1. to consume or use to no avail or profit. 2. to fail or neglect to use. 3. to destroy or consume gradually; wear away. 4. useless consumption or expenditure. 5. to kill or murder. 6. gradual impairment or decay. 7. devastation or ruin. 8. excrement.

Expanding Definitions Relating to Slavery:

During the slave trade, the Africans' lives were <u>wasted</u> once brought to America and sold into slavery. These humans thought to be "animals" did not live civilized, so they were taken from their homeland and brought here to put to good use. They were not considered human by the whites, they had no life. They <u>were used just like machines</u> (4) by working in fields or homes <u>to take money</u> (1) for the owner.

On the <u>exhausting trip</u> (3) over they were chained up in the bottom of the ship and crammed together for months. Eating mush when they were allowed, many would <u>starve to death and die</u> (5). Others would <u>die from diseases</u> (3) passed along through the ship. They would vomit on each other, live in each other's <u>bodily waste</u> (8) for the whole trip, and have to put up with the filthy rodents living in the ship with them. If someone died next to you, they would stay chained to you until they were thrown overboard.

Americans involved with the slave trade made a hefty profit off their new items of property and lived very nicely. While the slaves crowded in shacks eating what they could, before thrown out into the sun beaten fields for another day, and <u>tried to keep their culture alive</u> (3).

It was hard to keep their culture and spirits alive under such conditions. Both of these were also wasted. Once their soul died, they neglected their culture and <u>gave up on life all together</u> (1); therefore, they really were just bodies working as machines. <u>Over time their bodies were worn</u> (6) from the cruelty of the owners and the unforgiving weather. <u>Without a body, heart, and soul</u> (7), the slaves were ultimately useless and were left <u>totally neglected</u> (2) in a world of hatred and ignorance. Thousands of lives stolen and devastated by greed. It was a <u>waste</u> of flesh and blood.

---

student went through her writing and underlined and matched phrases to specific definitions. She put the number of the definition she felt related to her explanation of *waste* in the context of slavery.

CONCLUSION

This activity makes it very easy to assess the level of word concept knowledge students have acquired during a unit as well as their ability to use the shades of meaning the word contains. When the students go through their examples and decide which definition best fits what they are trying to express, they comment on the similarities and the differences in the definitions. They remember the shades of color and continue to expand their word knowledge because they used to think things were simple and limited, but now they know the concept of a word can be extensive and complex.

REFERENCE

Random House Webster's college dictionary. (1999). New York: Random House.

26

VERBAL TONE CHARADES

Cathy Blanchfield

I teach a tenth-grade class of gifted students in an inner-city school. Although these students are intelligent, most of them speak English as a second language so they still struggle with the nuances of the English language. One of my class goals is to ready the students for advanced placement courses in their junior and senior years. With this in mind, I can't be satisfied with merely introducing students to academic vocabulary; I must create activities that encourage them to understand the words at a deeper level.

A few years ago, I was struggling with helping my students understand an author's tone. They could pick up on the obvious tones: *positive* and *negative*; *suspicious* and *playful*; *sarcastic* and *humorous*. But qualities such as *menacing*, *reverent*, and *witty* they could not understand. As the school year was quickly coming to a close, I searched for one last lesson to give my students the experience of at least some of these more difficult concepts. That's when I began reading Carnicelli's *Words Work: Activities for Developing Vocabulary, Style, and Critical Thinking* (2001). One chapter is devoted to an activity he calls "Verbal Charades."

Carnicelli (2001) assigns groups of students an adjective, and each member of the group is asked to write a scenario or sketch that illustrates an adjective without actually using the assigned word. Although I have since taught the lesson using character traits and adjectives as he suggests, I have successfully adapted it for the concept of tone.

PROCEDURE

I begin by choosing a variety of words that my students might need for literary analysis in their advanced placement courses. Figure 26–1 is a list of such words. When I hand out one word to groups of four students, I allow them to discuss the word and its meaning. I want them to consider why authors might want to create this tone and what examples of movies and stories have been written in this tone. This discussion needs to be conducted away from the other groups so that they do not overhear each other's conversations and spoil the guessing of the charades later.

Next, each student is required to write a one-paragraph scenario in the tone assigned to the group. This often is the homework assignment. There should be no discussion between the students at this time because the greater the variation in scenario topics, the better it is for the game. I require that it is no longer than a page and does not use the assigned word in the scenario.

ambivalent	intellectual	passionate
amused	intriguing	remorseful
anxious	ironic	reverent
arrogant	irritated	sardonic
astonished	melancholy	satirical
competitive	menacing	sincere
critical	moral	skeptical
didactic	morose	solemn
hysterical	ominous	virtuous

FIGURE 26–1 Tone Vocabulary for Verbal Charades

When the students come back together, they share their four scenarios with the other group members. Group revisions take place at this time. Then the students decide in what order they will read the scenarios to the class. Carnicelli suggests that the scenarios should be read from the least obvious to the most obvious.

When the first student begins to read, I direct the class to listen for the tone of the paragraph. Then they are asked to write the tone that they heard on paper. After the second student reads, I ask the class to consider the tone that they wrote after the first reading and revise, if necessary. After the third scenario, the class again revises as necessary. After the fourth reading, I ask the students to share their final guesses. Although most times they do not guess the exact word I gave to the group, I list their guesses on the overhead projector. In the end we not only have a better understanding of the word, but we also have a list of close synonyms. Before we go on to the next group we discuss the similarities between the word that I assigned and all the words that the students guessed. They keep track of these synonyms for future work.

A group of students who had been assigned the word *menacing* began with a scenario of a bully who boasts, "I could end your so-called life with a snap of my finger." This elicited guesses such as *intimidation*, *aggressive*, and *threatening*. The next reader had written a poem that began with:

> *Lost in a place*
> *Dark, cold*
> *Only the light of the moon*

And ends with:

> *Even though it pushes you to strive*
> *It had you since the beginning*
> *It will finish you when the cloud covers the moon*
> *And the candle is blown out.*

The poem produced individual responses of *desperation*, *fearful*, and *evil*. The third scenario involved an erupting volcano blowing "ghastly smoke" and eventually erupting with "threatening power." Because the word *threatening* was used in this third scenario, many students who had guessed *threatening* after the second scenario had to change their guesses. In the end we had a list of many synonyms and associated words for the original word *menacing*.

After the students in each group read their scenarios, we have a list of eight or nine new words to describe tone as well as a variety of synonyms for these words. Figure 26–2 is a sample list of eight tone words and the student-generated synonyms. I then follow the activity with a set of poems or stories written in the tones we studied. Students are asked to analyze the new literature. They feel so much more successful because of their new arsenal of words.

FIGURE 26–2 Sample
Tone Words with Student-
Generated Synonyms

Assigned word	Student-generated synonyms
Menacing	intimidating, fearful, threatening
Ambivalent	uncertain, indecisive, conflicted, confused
Melancholy	sad, tragic, sorrowful, remorseful, mournful
Virtuous	ethical, moral, benevolent

CONCLUSION

I have used this technique each year while teaching the concept of tone to my students. Although it takes at least two days of instruction, it is well worth the time. Students need the time to process any concept and have a deep enough understanding of the word to use it in their own analysis.

I have also used this process with nongifted students in analyzing characters as Carnicelli presents it. It is an excellent activity for any age, as long as the choice of vocabulary is challenging, but not too difficult for the group. I have used words like *manipulative, courageous, spiritual, monstrous,* and *selfish* for character study. As the students write and then read the scenarios, students collect many synonyms and related words for each of my choices.

REFERENCE

Carnicelli, T. (2001). *Words work: Activities for developing vocabulary, style, and critical thinking.* Portsmouth, NH: Boynton/Cook.

Expanding Writing Vocabulary

Whenever students write, they need to have the vocabulary to express what they want to say. Students need to know the vocabulary that will speak to their audience, to understand the content vocabulary of their writing, and to choose the concise words to express their thoughts. It is not a true statement that many students cannot write, but what is true is that many students do not write well (The National Commission on Writing, 2003). This commission calls for many changes in schools to help students become more sophisticated writers. The Intersegmental Committee of the Academic Senates of the California Community Colleges, the California State University, and the University of California (2002) surveyed 289 college instructors concerning the most important literacy needs of incoming freshmen and found that 88 percent of the instructors thought "using vocabulary appropriate to college-level work and the discipline" (p. 22) was very important for college success.

Helping students choose vocabulary for creative writing is an English teacher's joy. Cathy Cirimele ("Learning the ABC's"), Malisa Ervin, Kathleen Markovich ("Recipe for Vocabulary"), and Jeffery Williams share ideas in this section that promote choosing varied and clear vocabulary in writing. The American Diploma

Project (2004) called for a more meaningful diploma by suggesting that before graduation, students need to "recognize nuances in the meanings of words; choose words precisely to enhance communication" (p. 31). These four lessons give students some of the tools they need to satisfy this standard.

Teachers understand that without content-specific vocabulary, students can't produce comprehensible subject-matter writing. "Good writers use language to express ideas, not simply describe events" (Conley, 2003, p. 15). With this in mind, Kathleen Markovich ("Curriculum-Related Word Banks") and Faith Nitschke have written activities that promote specific vocabulary for purpose and audience.

The *Academic Literacy* (Intersegmental Committee of the Academic Senates of the California Community Colleges, the California State University, and the University of California, 2002) document considers the knowledge and use of "academic English" an important need of students entering postsecondary education. They define this as " . . . complex sentence structures . . . and vocabulary appropriate for different kinds of writing" (p. 48). Cathy Cirimele ("The Excitement of Words"), Kathleen Markovich ("Don't Read This; It's Taboo") and Lisa Twiford all share ideas for complex sentence development and appropriate vocabulary for selected writing.

The activities in this section promote precise, clear vocabulary choice and academic writing in our secondary schools.

REFERENCES

American Diploma Project. (2004). *Ready or not: Creating a high school diploma that counts.* Washington, DC: Achieve.

Conley, D. T. (2003). *Understanding university success: A report from Standards for Success a project of the Association of American Universities and the Pew Charitable Trusts.* Eugene, OR: University of Oregon.

Intersegmental Committee of the Academic Senates of the California Community Colleges, the California State University, and the University of California. (2002). *Academic literacy: A statement of competencies expected of students entering California's public colleges and universities.* Sacramento, CA: Intersegmental Committee of the Academic Senates.

The National Commission on Writing in America's Schools and Colleges. (2003). *The neglected "R": The need for a writing revolution.* New York: The College Board.

Words: How a Writer "Paints" a Mood

27

Faith Nitschke

Teaching the concept of "mood" is somewhat challenging. Many teachers like to compare the idea of mood with the background music in movies or the compositional elements of painting, something most students are familiar with. For example, the cool colors and the calm sea in Mary Cassatt's "At the Beach" create its peaceful mood, and the suspenseful, repetitious, thump-thump-thump music of *Jaws* helps create its ominous mood. Students need to understand that there are a number of choices authors make as they work to achieve their purpose, including the selection of the topic and the specific events that occur in the text, the specific descriptions and details that are included in the text, their stance toward the topic, the sentence structure, and, as inferred above, the specific words selected that establish the text's mood.

This activity can help students, especially struggling students, to develop a better understanding of *mood*. Marzano, Pickering, and Pollock's (2001) research has shown that categorizing is a process that improves student learning and, in this case, helps students appreciate the deliberate choices authors make as they perfect a composition. This exercise is a perfect way to demonstrate to students the reading–writing connection by increasing the students' level of understanding about how authors write—specifically how authors make deliberate word choices in the drafting, revising, and editing stages. Students who grasp the significance of this deliberate word choice, which they should notice as readers, can then apply this concept to their own writing. It becomes a tool they can use as writers, especially in revision.

PROCEDURE

The following steps help students recognize how words shape mood:

1. Have students read and respond to a text using marginalia, having them also highlight words that strike them, puzzle them, or that they just like.
2. Have students share their written marginalia in small groups and as a whole group so that all students comprehend the text. The teacher may ask guiding questions and clarify unknown words, if necessary.
3. As a class, negotiate a working definition for *mood*. At this point, the class may or may not be ready to define the mood of the chosen text.
4. Have students each list at least 15 words that they think help establish the mood of the text. Struggling students and English Learners (EL) students may need to collaborate in this task, depending upon their level. Have students turn in these word lists to the teacher.

5. Type all the collected words into one table, one word per cell, eliminating any duplicate words by using the "sort" feature in the word processing program. Photocopy the final list for group work.
6. Put students in small groups and give each group a copy of the complete list. Have students cut the words apart and sort them in any way they wish. Then they give each sorted group of words a category label.
7. Have each group copy their sorted words and category labels onto a transparency and share their transparencies with the class.
8. After groups have shared their sorts, have the class negotiate a final sort and category labels. A sample of a class sort for carter's "Mama's Cupboard" (1986) is provided in Figure 27–1.

Category: **bad things** wart cramped plywood dark ugly broken dry	Category: **pantry** delicacies never came out again dark crowded pantry cramped never ate new supplies arrived	guests guests never came weak-tea-stained-plywood veneer wonderful with its bounty and visions having dreams for dinner
Category: **words that bring forth images** smoked meats stacking dolls Almond Roca childhood home sardines church oysters peanuts salmon pecans beef stew popcorn kernels mandarin orange clam chowder segments gum cherries apricot nectar pretzels shoestring potatoes	Category: **negative words** broken dreams cramped sound shaking crowded sneak longingly no one was ever invited dark broken ugly never ate anything	
Category: **things in your head** dreams illusions fantasies	Category: **children** broken dreams denials promise never came illusion stop believing never ate	
Category: **words that had no meaning or didn't know what to do with** threats explicit focal general benefits goodies	Category: **what the kids did or wanted** bounty awaited faith visions dreamed treat ceremoniously arrive promise	
Category: **fun stuff** birthday party	Category: **nice things** church donated good faith	

FIGURE 27–1   Student-Selected Words Used in "Mama's Cupboard" That Set Mood or Bring Forth Imagery

Use the appropriate categories to negotiate a description of the mood of the text, citing which words contribute to this mood (if the class was unable to do this in Step 3). Be explicit about how to express a statement about mood in academic language. The teacher may wish to model what this would look like with a statement such as, "The author creates a depressing or negative mood by her use of words such as *broken dreams* or *cramped*." For EL students, the teacher may wish to counter the words that created the mood with other words that mean the opposite so that students see the way these sets of words oppose each other. For example, the class may negotiate that the opposite of *broken dreams* is *wonderful dreams* or *dreams that came true*. Marzano (2004) supports the activity of using word opposites to increase student learning.

EXAMPLES

The examples in Figure 27–1 come from Barbara Carter's essay, "Mama's Cupboard." In this essay, Carter, in a very nonsentimental tone, describes her mother's pantry that was filled with an array of delicious treats. The children were never given any of these treats because the mother felt that none of them were ever good enough to deserve a treat. Not all of the words and categories the students selected related to mood, which is good because they lead to rich discussions about other reasons why and how authors make deliberate decisions in selecting the words of their composition. For example, the class had an in-depth, analytical discussion of why they thought Carter (1986) named the specific items in "words that bring forth images." They realized that there was something there each of them really liked, and this was a way the author grabbed their attention or "hooked" them into the essay. This led to a discussion of why imagery is important in effective writing and why, in revision, it is important to include descriptions and details in their own writing if they omitted these in their first drafts or to find places where they may need to elaborate. Students now understand what it means when a teacher writes "needs more details" in the margin. These discussions also provide a means to expand students' background knowledge about a variety of vocabulary in general.

CONCLUSION

Some of my students' sorting is imperfect, but my struggling students' awareness of the specific power and function of words was heightened by this exercise. After the students studied how writers made conscious decisions about the words they used, they expressed more concern about the words they were using in their compositions. They substituted words in revision. They asked how to use a thesaurus. When given a prompt as a posttest that required them to analyze the mood and purpose of a different essay, they applied what they had learned and began their process by marking words in the text. This exercise left them much better equipped to address writing tasks that ask them to analyze how an author achieves his or her purpose. They are also equipped to be more astute readers of texts, taking note of the ways different authors create the mood they want readers to feel through the specific words chosen.

REFERENCES

Carter, B. (1986). Mama's cupboard. *Student writers at work.* New York: St. Martin's Press.

Marzano, R. J. (2004). *Building background knowledge.* Alexandria, VA: Association for Supervision and Curriculum Development.

Marzano, R. J., Pickering, D. J., & Pollock, J. E. (2001). *Classroom instruction that works: Research-based strategies for increasing student achievement.* Alexandria, VA: Association for Supervision and Curriculum Development.

28

LEARNING THE ABC's

Cathy Cirimele

Teaching students vocabulary can be more engaging if words are presented in the context of creative writing. Creating alphabet books is one such activity. Even though this is an assignment I give primarily in my writing classes, it is easily adaptable to any course when teaching vocabulary. I use it to teach alliteration and the use of words in new and interesting ways, but it is applicable to any set of words. I know teachers who have used alphabet books to teach a foreign language as well as in math and science classes. In any class, the books then become a resource of vocabulary and word arrangements for future writing assignments.

Teenagers, in particular, seem to enjoy reading children's books, especially those that they recognize from their childhood. I have built a classroom library of over 50 children's books, and I use them whenever I can as a means of approaching ideas in a way that is not often present in a high school classroom. As an example of what this assignment could look like when it is completed, I read my students various alphabet books, including Graeme Base's *Animalia* (1987). In particular, it has wonderful, colorful illustrations and the word choices are both sophisticated and unique.

PROCEDURE

The assignment is to create an alphabet book. Some students have created a cookbook; others have used alliteration as Base does; and still others have used themes such as colors, games, or flowers. It is often helpful to keep samples of alphabet books and other sources on hand, such as *The Scholastic Rhyming Book* (Young, 1994). The only requirement is that they must illustrate all 26 letters of the alphabet, even though not every letter needs to cover an entire page. It is important to give students the opportunity either to illustrate their alphabet book themselves or, if they do not feel particularly adept at drawing, to cut out pictures or use computer graphics as illustrations. I do not want them to feel intimidated by the examples; rather, I want to expose them to the wide variety of alphabet books available. The books students in my creative writing class create will be read to kindergarten students at a neighboring school, so I remind students that they need to limit the number of words on a page and to make the illustrations colorful and bold. Often I will show them children's books with abstract designs that create an impression rather than a literal rendering of ideas (see the page of one student's book in Figure 28–1).

Because one of my purposes is to demonstrate how effective alliterative language can be, each letter of the alphabet must be illustrated with words that begin with the letter they are representing. Of course, some exceptions can be made in

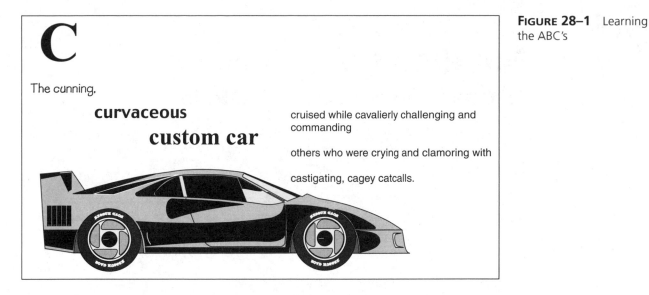

FIGURE 28–1 Learning the ABC's

C

The cunning,

curvaceous

custom car

cruised while cavalierly challenging and commanding

others who were crying and clamoring with

castigating, cagey catcalls.

order to create a sentence that makes sense, although nonsense sentences can also be fun if they are done effectively.

When they are completed, the books are bound with brads, yarn, or in any other way that keeps the book collated and portable. Often, I will have the book pages laminated at a nominal price at our district's instructional media center. This assures some level of durability, especially if my students choose to leave the alphabet books with the kindergarten children after they read to them.

The books must be presented to others. If we are going to read to young children, I set aside some practice time in class for students to read to each other. Of course, I have modeled this by reading alphabet books to them and by discussing the different approaches primary teachers use when reading to children. If we are sharing the books in class, students read to each other in groups, and then each group picks a book to be shared with the entire class. When we do share the alphabet books with the kindergarten children, we read the books and then have a pizza party. As the students and the children are reading and then playing together, the kindergarten teacher and I take photos, which we later put on posters to hang in both classrooms. Often, my students will leave the books for the children to continue to read and perhaps even keep in the classroom for the rest of the school year.

CONCLUSION

This lesson is both fun and instructive. By writing their own alphabet book, students are allowed to play with language and use words in unique and interesting ways. Although they are also learning how to use alliteration, it becomes almost secondary to the larger task of using words to create meaning. By sharing their books with young children, they are once again privy to the wonder and joy of reading a book for both pleasure and instruction. It is a lesson that many of them remember and often becomes one of their favorite assignments in the class. It is truly a lesson that almost every student enjoys and remembers.

REFERENCES

Base, G. (1987). *Animalia*. New York: Abrams.

Young, S. (2006). *The Scholastic rhyming book*. New York: Scholastic.

29

NURTURING MY STUDENTS' ROMANCE WITH WORDS

Malisa Ervin

After reading "A Love of Words" from Ralph Fletcher's *What a Writer Needs* (1993), I found myself struck with a sense of mourning for some of the students I teach. Fletcher spoke of words and how he would collect words that he found interesting and bank them for later use. His love of words was so obvious; he reminded me of my old fascination with language, how I was in awe of the way words were put together by Fitzgerald, Tan, and others. I knew that many of my students did not share this love of language. In my first year of teaching I was disappointed that the majority of students preferred "The Crucible" to *The Great Gatsby*. Certainly, "The Crucible" is a fine play, but as far as beauty of language is concerned, *The Great Gatsby* is vastly superior.

> And as the moon rose higher the inessential houses began to melt away until gradually I became aware of the old island here that flowered once for Dutch sailors' eyes—a fresh green breast of the new world. Its vanished trees, the trees that had made way for Gatsby's house, had once pandered in whispers to the last and greatest of all human dreams; for a transitory enchanted moment man must have held his breath in the presence of this continent, compelled into an aesthetic contemplation he neither understood nor desired, face to face for the last time in history with something commensurate to his capacity for wonder. . . . Gatsby believed in the green light, the orgiastic future that year by year recedes before us. It eluded us then, but that's no matter—tomorrow we will run faster, stretch out our arms farther. . . . And one fine morning—So we beat on, boats against the current, borne back ceaselessly into the past. (Fitzgerald, 1992, p. 182)

Somehow I felt I had failed Fitzgerald by not getting my students to love his words, by not getting them to revere him for his ability to capture such complex emotions so poetically and accurately.

Later in my career, an English language learner of mine remembered the meaning of the word *revere* when I was working with my class. He reminded the class of the word's meaning from a discussion of an episode from *The Joy Luck Club* (Tan, 1989) that we had read the previous year. I was shocked. Not only did this student make a connection that I had not remembered, but he recalled the specific instance the word *revere* was used in an extremely difficult, complex novel. My only explanation is that he must have loved that word when he first heard it. He understood that it was the perfect word for the situation. Thus, deep down, students do have a love for language, but too often this love manifests itself simply as a brief flirtation and not as anything long-lasting.

People have a natural love for language, but in today's bottom-line world, this love is being stifled by the need to know and know fast. The popularity of soundbytes is one strong example of this phenomenon. It was reported that the 2000 presidential debates between Gore and Bush were rated at a seventh-grade level in use of vocabulary, and that this degradation is also occurring in television and print media. Rarely does anyone listen to a speech with simple appreciation of the orator's art; they want the down-and-dirty facts, not aesthetics. Thus, it has become evident that as a teacher, I must nurture my students' romance with words. I must take the time to show students my own passion for words in the hopes that it will ignite others. I must take the time to read and write poetry. More important, I must share my writing with my students and demonstrate where I am particularly proud of my use of a specific word. Students also need to be given time to play with words; they must be encouraged to collect words and claim ownership of them. They must be given a variety of opportunities to write in many genres.

PROCEDURE

The first step in the process of nurturing students' love for language is giving them an appreciation of words. This is accomplished by having students maintain a personal word bank of words they have come across through literature, music, television, or conversation that were particularly interesting, funny, intriguing, or confusing. My students keep a notebook that serves as their reading journal. They turn the notebook upside down and begin the word wall on the last page. In this way, they always have their word wall with their reading journal and should they run out of room, they simply turn the page and continue. It is vital that students write a brief note about the situation in which the word was encountered or a situation in which the word could be used. For example, one student shared *exsanguination*; immediately, all the other students wanted to know what the word meant. After the student explained it, I commented that it would be perfect for a vampire or science fiction story. This connection would be noted in their list. Figure 29–1 is an excerpt from a student's personal word bank.

Next, students must be given opportunities to employ the words in their banks. Occasionally, I have the students create a story or poem, incorporating a

FIGURE 29–1 Student Word Bank

Word Bank

exsanguinate—to drain or lose blood (Vampire or sci-fi story)

cell—a small group working as a unit in a larger organization (Spy or espionage story)

troglodyte—a member of primitive people dwelling in caves (Use as an insult in any story)

instigate—to start something or get something going (Mystery)

petulantly—rudely (This would be good to help develop a character's personality or mood in a scene.)

sarcastically—saying something with sarcasm, stinging remarks meant to ridicule a person, institution, or ideas (This would be good to add description to a character's tone toward someone or something in the story.)

zealot—a fanatical person who gives blind, unreasonable loyalty to a group (Use in a piece about terrorism.)

peril—danger (Spy, mystery, or action story)

minimum of 10 words from their banks. Other times, I assign students a specific genre to write and challenge them to include words from their banks. There are so many possibilities. A colleague of mine suggested pulling words from writing, looking them up in the thesaurus, discussing the nuances of each word found, and then making a decision about which word works best. This kind of activity gets at the heart of making students understand that writers make conscious decisions about the words they choose and that the right word is very powerful. With this goal in mind, I often point out interesting word choices in essays and analyze how the word choice furthers the author's message.

CONCLUSION

The preceding activities are all designed to give students an appreciation for words and to make them aware of writers' choices so that as writers, they can make informed decisions. No matter what else I may do for my students, I do not think I will be truly happy until I can see growing evidence that they love words and language. I fear a world in which we have lost hundreds of thousands of words from our working vocabularies; so many students and adults miss the nuances in a specific choice of a word or the poetic beauty in how an idea is conveyed through language. I hope we teachers and lovers of language can stem the tide and reinvigorate this world with the vibrancy of the perfect word choice and one's capacity for wonder.

REFERENCES

Fitzgerald, F. (1992). *The great Gatsby*. New York: Macmillan.
Fletcher, R. (1993). *What a writer needs*. Portsmouth, NH: Heinemann.
Tan, A. (1989). *The joy luck club*. New York: Ivy Books.

INTEGRATING CREATIVE VERBS INTO STUDENT WRITING

Jeffery Williams

The presence of elevated diction in our students' writing signals their growing maturity. However, my initial attempts to motivate students to raise the level of their diction failed miserably; students would dutifully grab a thesaurus, and then create sentences such as the following: "The ostentatious man was vituperative a lot around his wife." I nearly gave up the idea as sound in theory but useless in practice. But then I realized, through observing the craft of gifted writers, that the creatively used verb is a more successful and less intrusive means of expressing the voice of the writer. I discovered that developing word banks for students could help them practice varying the words they use more subtly and creatively. Figure 30–1 shows some examples of student-revised sentences incorporating thoughtfully chosen verbs.

PROCEDURE

The verb bank I use in class emerged through the last few years of lessons (see Figure 30–2). After handing out my verb list, which contains several categories, I instruct students to peruse the list and highlight words they like and would try to integrate in their writing. During brainstorming, they write down other words that come to mind in the categories. In small groups, students share words and jot down the ones they appreciate. We share from among the best in class. Depending on the strength of the class, I will read a poem or a narrative passage and have students analyze the effectiveness of the verb usage. I particularly like Dorianne Laux's poem "Two Pictures of My Sister" (1990); for lower-level classes, I select excerpts from a Stephen King short story, "Battleground" (1976). We generally conclude that familiar language, creatively used, is better appreciated than an overuse of, as Ernest Hemingway once said, 10-dollar words. We also note that many nouns in the gloriously messy English language have evolved into verbs.

I then assign a short narrative or poem, asking students to incorporate two or three verbs from the bank. I emphasize avoiding wordiness. I remind them that one well-chosen word is more respected than an insistence on multiple words and I proclaim the adage "Half of art is knowing when to stop" (Arthur William Radford). Another idea is to instruct students to use the verbs of one subject area to describe an unrelated scene or situation. We go from having students read examples of their work in small groups to sharing with the entire class.

I usually introduce this lesson at the beginning of the school year and tell students to keep the bank for reference, because I often require that they incorporate a few of the verbs in each significant writing assignment—whether it be a narrative or an expository essay.

FIGURE 30–1 Student
Examples of Verb Lesson

Before/After Sentences

Before

Emily Grierson's father didn't let her go out of the house, which stopped her from being with friends and suitors.

After

Emily Grierson's father cloistered her from the everyday activities of the town, robbing her of all social life.

Before

My mother is always after me about cleaning my room and doing my homework.

After

My mother badgers me about cleaning my room and completing my homework.

Before

Controversial issues such as abortion or capital punishment tend to pull apart people and groups.

After

Controversial issues such as abortion or capital punishment tend to polarize people and groups.

Before

The tumor grew deeper into the brain, taking away the patient's ability to care for himself.

After

The tumor webbed through his brain, eroding the patient's ability to care for himself.

FIGURE 30–2 Student
Verb List

Integrate creative verbs into your writing

Utilize the following list as a word bank to raise the level of your writing and forever destroy your overindulgence in dead, overused verbs.

Verbs connected to war
1. sabotage—to do harm to something, to destroy
2. camouflage—to mask, disguise, or conceal one's appearance, feelings, or motives
3. trigger—to activate, set off, or initiate (as in an event)
4. ambush—to attack from a concealed position
5. flank or counterattack—to put on each side, or to circle around and attack
6. slaughter, butcher, or decimate—to kill large numbers in a cruel fashion
7. dynamite—to detonate, to explode
8. surrender—to give up or concede
9. march or parade—to traverse at an orderly, regulated pace
10. marshal—to enlist, organize, or guide
11. torpedo or dive-bomb—to destroy decisively
12. execute—to put to death
13. boomerang—to backfire or result in an adverse effect upon the originator

FIGURE 30–2 Continued

14. combat or battle or duel—to engage in attack
15. courtmartial—to try by military tribunal
16. bayonet—to prod, stab, or kill with a sharp weapon

Verbs connected to nautical terms

17. pilot—to steer or control the course of
18. anchor—providing stability or support
19. navigate—to control the course of, follow a plan
20. tether—to restrict or bind, to secure (also—moor)
21. harbor—to keep, protect, nourish, give shelter to
22. broadside—to attack by surprise, verbally or physically
23. jettison—to abandon or discard things
24. mothball—to dismantle a structure, vehicle, or system
25. capsize—to overturn a boat
26. chart (a course)—to make plans
27. pirate—to seize or steal, reproduce, or make use of another's work illicitly

Verbs connected to tools

28. plumb—to examine or study closely, think deeply about
29. hone—to sharpen, give an edge to, narrow one's focus (also—hew)
30. hammer—to deal repeated blows, to work diligently, or to criticize
31. yoke—to harness, fit into labor
32. shovel—to clear, throw, or convey
33. wrench—to pull free, to injure
34. drill—to make a hole, to hit, to instruct
35. axe—(also—thatchet, machete, knife) to remove ruthlessly
36. chisel—to shape, to cheat, to intrude
37. nail—to hit, seize, master, win
38. scissor—to cut or clip

Verbs connected to farming

39. plow or furrow—to proceed laboriously, to form a driving force
40. prune—to remove or cut away to improve growth
41. cultivate—to grow, tend, refine, (also—nurture and foster)
42. glean—to collect or gather
43. harvest—to gather, to reap
44. mow—to cut, destroy, or overwhelm
45. rooted—to become firmly established, or to be removed (rooted out)

Verbs connected to fishing

46. angling—to fish for, to attempt to catch, to seek something
47. lure—to entice, bait, or attract with a view to catch
48. net—to catch or ensnare
49. bait, cast, hook, reel, land, trawl—process of fishing
50. gut, flay, scale—process of cleaning fish

Verbs connected to religion

51. cloister—to seclude or shut away from society
52. kowtow—to worship or bow down to
53. pontificate—to express one's opinion in a self-righteous, proud manner
54. resurrect—to bring back to life, use, or prominence
55. crucify—to unjustly, either verbally or physically, attack someone
56. canonize—to treat as sacred, to glorify, to declare a saint
57. defrock—to remove a minister's credentials due to wrongdoing
58. meditate—to engage in contemplation, to introspect
59. preach—to deliver a sermon on moral instruction

FIGURE 30–2 Continued

60. blaspheme—to speak against God in an irreverent manner
61. baptize—to initiate, to cleanse
62. herald—to usher in, proclaim, or announce

Verbs created from animal characteristics

63. wolf (down)—to eat ravenously, voraciously
64. parrot—to imitate or copy one's actions or words (also—ape and mimic)
65. spider—to invade or infiltrate
66. dovetail—to combine or interlock harmoniously
67. badger—to persistently harass or pester someone
68. buffalo—to intimidate by forceful words or physical presence
69. hound—to pursue closely or watch one's actions persistently (also—dog)
70. hawk—to peddle or attempt to sell
71. fish—to search or hunt for something
72. pigeonhole—to classify, categorize, or stereotype by appearance
73. lionize—to treat as a celebrity, king of the jungle
74. cow—to frighten with threats or a show of force
75. ferret (out)—to uncover and bring to light by searching
76. chicken (out)—to act in a cowardly manner, to lose one's nerve
77. snake—to move snakelike, to worm into a conversation, break into a building
78. monkey (around) or horse (around)—to indulge in idle play, goofing off, horseplay
79. dog—worn out by work
80. bulldog or bulldoze—acting stubborn or to bully, act in a cruel manner
81. weasel—to back out of a commitment or agreement in a sneaky or cowardly manner
82. birddog—to follow closely or monitor
83. leapfrog—to advance forward in progress, avoiding a roundabout route
84. flounder—to move clumsily or in confusion

Verbs connected to music, dance, and art

85. orchestrate—to arrange or compose music for a performance
86. harmonize—to provide a pleasing combination of sounds to the melody
87. trumpet—to proclaim or praise something with excitement and pride
88. drum—to tap rhythmically, but also to make known, to expel, or to devise
89. conduct—to direct the course of, manage, or control
90. compose—to create a musical piece, but also to calm oneself or reconcile
91. polish—to make smooth and shiny
92. sculpt—to shape, mold, or fashion with artistry and precision
93. embroider or quilt—to add embellishments
94. crescendo—to reach a point of great intensity, force, or volume
95. sashay—to strut or flounce in a showy manner
96. vault—to jump or leap over

Verbs connected to clothing or appearance

97. cotton (to or up)—to become friendly or agreeable
98. tailor—to adapt or alter
99. collar—to seize or detain
100. straitjacket—to constrict
101. fashion or style—to design
102. hem—to surround and shut in (also—enclose, encase, engulf)
103. shroud—to cut off from sight

Verbs connected to computer age

104. network—to develop contacts in order to exchange information, share responsibilities
105. interface—to interact or coordinate smoothly

FIGURE 30–2   Continued

106. short-circuit—to hamper progress, malfunction
107. download—to transfer data or programs through a computer
108. surf (the net)—to browse or peruse the Internet
109. crash (system)—to lose vital functions of a computer
110. freeze—to lose computer operation through system paralysis
111. boot—to start up a computer

Verbs connected to writing

112. limn—to describe or depict in art—such as painting, sculpture, or words
113. parse—to break down into components with an explanation of form, function, or syntax
114. journal—to reflect in a stream-of-consciousness form of writing
115. chronicle—to record historical events in prose form
116. pen—to write or author

Verbs connected to functions of the body

117. paralyze—to impair functions, make inoperative
118. hamstring—to cripple or hinder
119. bruise—to hurt or injure
120. lacerate—to mangle, tear, cause, emotional pain
121. amputate—to cut away or remove a limb
122. suffocate—to stifle or suppress, to asphyxiate
123. muscle—to use force
124. handcuff—to restrain, immobilize (also—imprison, chain, manacle)

Verbs connected to business and industry

125. calibrate—to make corrections, adjust
126. ignite—to kindle an emotion, a cause, or embroil in conflict
127. refine—to make better
128. formulate—to devise or invent
129. negotiate—to sell, to succeed in accomplishing, to manage
130. capsulize—to condense or summarize
131. prefabricate (fabricate as well)—to make up or construct in an unoriginal manner
132. pioneer—to explore unknown territory, or establish a new theory or innovation, trailblaze
133. wrest—to obtain control by force (as in a hostile takeover)
134. augment—to increase or enlarge in size or stature
135. oscillate—to waver back and forth, to vacillate between two choices

Nouns created into verbs

136. feather—to gain wealth, accomplish an achievement, to decorate
137. pillory—to ridicule, lampoon, or satirize
138. dwarf—to make small by comparison
139. spruce—to make more attractive with decorations or embellishments
140. jawbone—to persuade or pressure with verbal arguments
141. champion—to support a cause passionately, to advocate for the needs of someone
142. pine—to desire, long for
143. jade—to become insensitive, cynical, or skeptical towards the good things in life
144. cloud—to confuse or puzzle
145. milk—to extract or to use for one's own benefit
146. weather—to pass through safely, survive, endure successfully
147. pepper—to pelt or shower with speech or weapons
148. mirror—to faithfully reflect an image or model
149. shadow—to follow after, to trail, generally in secret
150. ground—to supply essential information, instruct in fundamentals (also—school)
151. siphon—to deplete of resources
152. prostitute—to sell oneself for an unworthy purpose

FIGURE 30–2   Continued

Other creative verbs

153. polarize—to separate, pull apart, sever relations
154. stonewall—to delay or stall the beginning of something
155. pander—to cater to people's baser, physical desires for profit (prostitution, alcohol)
156. propel—to advance forward or upward
157. metamorphose—to transform in appearance, form, or character
158. nestle—to settle in comfortably, cocoon in a place
159. evolve—to develop gradually
160. entice—to lure or arouse passions or desires
161. erode—to wear away, slowly crumble, and disintegrate
162. relish—to take pleasure in, to fully enjoy
163. regale—to entertain with jokes, stories, music, etc.
164. sponge—to habitually rely on others for money, food, or shelter
165. bruit—to spread news of, repeat
166. amplify or magnify or elevate—to make larger or more powerful
167. alienate—to estrange, dissociate, or exile
168. abort—to terminate, (also—miscarry)
169. energize—to activate, invigorate with power
170. masquerade—to wear a disguise, put on a deceptive appearance
171. cascade—to fall
172. treasure, cherish, embrace—to value or appreciate
173. espouse/estrange—to give one's loyalty in a relationship or to a cause/to alienate a relationship
174. divorce—to separate or disunite

CONCLUSION

The verb bank gives students a needed resource for elevated diction. Although some students may overuse the new verbs initially, with time and practice, most come to understand that a few strategically placed verbs from our bank add images and action to their writing. These additions ultimately improve the sound of their writing.

REFERENCES

King, S. (1976). *Night shift*. New York: Signet.
Laux, D. (1990). *Awake*. New York: Boa Edition.

RECIPE FOR VOCABULARY: SHORT-STORY THREE-LAYER CAKE WITH CHOCOLATE FROSTING

Kathleen Markovich

The purpose of this multilayered assignment is multiple exposures: Students consciously review and consult a list of unfamiliar words until the words become familiar. The students select these words from their independent reading and record them in response journals as vocabulary entries; that's layer one. Next, they each teach one word to the class using a vocabulary graphic. The graphics are posted in the classroom, and the students write the list of student-taught words in their journals; that's layer two. For the short story layer, they use 15 to 20 of the words to compose their own piece of fiction, and they complete a check of how well they used the words during a peer response activity. After that, they revise and write final drafts of their short stories. Finally, as frosting, volunteers read their stories to the class for extra credit and someone wins a prize. Students see, hear, and read the words over and over as they progress through the layers of this assignment; this process helps them move words from their reading to their writing vocabulary.

LAYER ONE: INDEPENDENT READING AND RESPONSE JOURNALS

In the third quarter, while my classes are reading plays, their homework is to read a book of their own choice. My classes are divided into acting companies for reading and performing the plays, and I instruct them to preview and review as homework, but we all know that they probably don't read or reread the plays when they go home. I want them to have homework every night, so I assign independent reading to make sure they read and write while we read two or three plays during class.

Before they select their independent reading books, we go to the library for a book talk given by our librarian, and I talk about some of the books I keep in the classroom for students to check out. I set a deadline for them to have a book, and on that day, I pass around a sign-up sheet so I get a list of their choices, and I go over the reading response journal assignment. While they are reading, they stop 10 times to write two types of journal entries: a literature response and a vocabulary response. As I explain the journal entries, I ask the students to divide the total number of pages in their book by 10. I explain, "If your book has 185 pages, you will stop every 19 pages for your journal entries. If your book has 223 pages, you will stop every 22 pages."

The literature response is the typical one. Each time students stop for a literary response, they select one of these: (1) a significant passage they copy, with the page number, followed by an explanation of why the passage is important; (2) an analytical response, in which they discuss what they observe about symbols, characters, writer's style, theme, parallel or recurring events, connections to literature we have read previously; (3) a personal response connecting the text to their lives or feelings.

My students are familiar with these literature responses because, by the third quarter, we have completed two core novels and have written different types of response journals for both of them. Because we have studied two novels, they are familiar, to varying degrees, with literary terms and the elements of fiction—information they will need for the last layer of this assignment.

For their vocabulary entries, I explain, "Select a word you don't know or are unsure of. The vocabulary response includes the word and the number of the page on which it is found, the context (the sentence from the book or, if the sentence is long, then the five words before and after the word), and the correct dictionary definition."

"What if there are no words I don't know?"

"Then you need to select a different book. Push yourself; choose a more difficult book," is my response to that student question. Our school purchased the Accelerated Reader program, so some of our library books have the rating labels on their spines; the Accelerated Reader list is available on our library's computers. Our librarian has compiled a reading list for college-bound students, and I can also help students select books that will challenge their intellects. "The point is to locate a book that is challenging, that contains a few words you don't know," I tell my classes.

Students then have five weeks to read their books and complete their journals. In the meantime, we begin class each day with book talks about our reading choices, then we work on the plays we are reading and performing. I also check journals occasionally to make sure students are progressing with this portion of the assignment.

About two weeks into the assignment, I check their vocabulary choices and add the "teach-a-word" and the short-story layers to the assignment. I tell them to be careful about the words they select because they will be teaching one of their words to the class. "You will be making a vocabulary graphic and taking notes on all the words selected by this class. Then you will be using the words to write your own short story—so make sure you select words that other students will want to use."

LAYER TWO: CREATING VOCABULARY GRAPHICS AND TEACHING THE WORDS

Once the independent reading and journals are completed, the students select one of their 10 words to teach to the class. I explain that they will make a graphic and teach the word, that everyone will be taking notes as they teach, and that the assignment after all the words are taught is to use 15 to 20 words—the larger the class, the longer the list, and the more words I require—in a short story they create. To help them select "good" words to teach each other, I throw in the frosting: When the final drafts are due, students can volunteer to read their stories aloud for two points of extra credit, and we will keep track of which words the students use. A prize will go to the student whose word is used the most. This gives the students criteria for selecting their words and motivation for doing a good job of teaching them.

To create the vocabulary graphic, ask students to include the following elements: the word, the part of speech, the definition, a sentence, and a graphic that illustrates the definition. I have students use 8 ½ × 11-inch paper because a) we need room for three class sets of these graphics on the classroom walls, and b) students spend too much time creating the graphic if it is larger. Time is precious in the third quarter; it's when we realize the days taken from instruction for the mandated testing will make it impossible to complete all the teaching and learning necessary for our students to do well on the mandated tests. Consequently, my instructions for teaching the word are brief and concise:

1. Write the word on the board.
2. Say the word.
3. Show the graphic.

4. Give the part of speech and the definition.
5. Read the sentence.
6. Explain the graphic.
7. Say the word again.

These directions are written on a piece of 12 × 18-inch construction paper and are taped to a student desk so that students facing the class can read the directions right in front of them. After many years of teaching, I finally learned to stop writing the instructions on the board, because the students turn to the board to see what they need to do, and then they teach with their backs to the class. Taping the instructions to a desk solves this problem.

We teach the words in alphabetical order—though I don't announce that until the day we teach our words because students will select *w*, *x*, *y*, and *z* words if they know this in advance. Earlier in the week, I pass around a list of names and ask students to write the words they selected to teach next to their names. From this list, I can check for duplicates and make changes in advance, and I can ask student aides to create an alphabetical list for me, although I don't call out the list. Instead, we work through the alphabetical order as a class—the process of figuring out who goes next keeps students engaged and on their toes, just the way I like them.

After the presentations—students staple the vocabulary graphic up on the bulletin board, leaving spaces for absentees. Alphabetical order helps students refer to their lists as they work through the rest of the assignment. While each student is teaching a word, the other students are taking notes in their journals by writing down each word, its part of speech, and the definition.

To give you an idea of the kinds of words students select, Figure 31–1 contains the list for English II P and English II GATE; English II is tenth-grade English, and a "P" class is a college preparatory class, which is the level for everyone who is not in GATE (Gifted and Talented) or honors classes.

LAYER THREE: THE WRITING PROCESS FOR THE SHORT STORIES

After all the words have been taught, I hand out the peer response sheet shown in Figure 31–2. I generally hand out peer response sheets and scoring rubrics when making assignments; this clarifies the purpose, the components, and the evaluation criteria for the assignment. The purpose here is twofold: vocabulary building and familiarity with the elements of fiction. I tell my students they do not need to use every element of fiction—four is a good number. Every story, however, has to have conflict of some kind; no conflict means no story. For this particular assignment, I use the peer response sheet as the tool for evaluation.

Now, the students' homework is reviewing their vocabulary lists and incorporating 15 to 20 words—the bigger the class, the higher the number—in a short story of their own creation. I do allow them to change the forms of the words because I want them to learn how to manipulate the words to fit their stories and sentences. I give them a week to produce a legible draft, with all the vocabulary words underlined, for peer response. I don't know how many times students review the vocabulary list as they write the story, but the more times, the better.

On peer response day, I give each student two copies of the peer response sheet. They copy their vocabulary words in the grid provided, then exchange stories and one peer response sheet with another student. Their instructions are to read the story twice: the first time to check the vocabulary, and the second time to respond to the elements of fiction. During that first reading, they code each vocabulary word according to Step 1 for the peer responder: check mark, if the word is used correctly; question mark, if they're not sure; and circle the words used incorrectly. I caution students to be aware of parts of speech and how the writer uses the vocabulary words. Are the adjectives used as adjectives, the verbs as verbs? This

Figure 31–1 Student-
Selected Vocabulary List
from English II P and
English II GATE

English II P Vocabulary List

acquiesced	martyr
barricade	overwrought
bludgeoned	pandemonium
chiffon	palpitating
contingent	paltry
covetously	paragon
crusade	peremptorily
denuded	pinnacle
emblazoned	relinquished
grudgingly	swoon
hallooing	transgress
immensity	tyrannical
lethargical	usurped

Vocabulary List for English II GATE

acquiesce	malevolent
agglutination	mediocrity
copiously	mellifluous
disseminate	ostracized
enigmatical	palpitating
exuding	palsied
fluctuating	pretensions
hyperbole	sobriquet
incognito	ubiquitous
inevitability	upbraided
inkling	vestibule
interminable	vociferating
lucid	volition

is a good time to talk about syntax and word order and how words function in English sentences. For the second reading, they are to respond to items two through six, which relate to the elements of fiction.

After the first round of peer responses, each student exchanges a clean peer response sheet and his or her story with another student and completes the process a second time. While they are reading each other's stories, their journals are out and they are checking the words and definitions they recorded earlier—alphabetical order for teaching the words is important during this step of the process. Here they are reviewing their vocabulary lists again.

I caution my students that peer response is extremely important. As writers, they depend on each other for accurate and useful peer response. I model and provide examples. I actively teach peer response as an important and necessary part of the writing process. When I evaluate their writing, I evaluate the peer response, too. If a vocabulary word is used incorrectly, I check to see that the peer responders alerted the writer to a problem. If the peer responders did their jobs, they get full credit. If the peer responders led the writer astray—didn't alert him/her to a problem—then they, as well as the writer, will lose points. Peer response rounds are worth five points each, and I generally make the products of the writing process worth at least 50 percent of the points. Completing only a final draft—and skipping the writing process—nets a student no more than 50 percent, which is a failing grade.

When both rounds of peer response are finished, we go over revision. I explain that they need to try to use the vocabulary words correctly, paying special attention to the words their peer responders coded with a question mark or a circle. They need to read over the comments and evaluations of their use of the elements of

FIGURE 31–2 Peer
Response Sheet

Vocabulary Short Story   Story by _____

Peer Response by _____ Date _____ Per. _____

Purpose: 1. Practice using new vocabulary words correctly

2. Demonstrate growing understanding of the elements of fiction

Writer:

1.   Make sure your ____ vocabulary words are all underlined.
2.   In the space below, list the vocabulary words you used in your story.

1.	11.
2.	12.
3.	13.
4.	14.
5.	15.
6.	16.
7.	17.
8.	18.
9.	19.
10.	20.

Peer Responder:

1.   In the list above, code each vocabulary word from the story:
   ✔ Check the words you're sure are used correctly
   ? Question mark words you're not sure about
   O Circle the words you're sure are NOT used correctly

2.   Does the story have an eye-catching and meaningful title?   Yes   No
       Suggest another title:

3.   What point of view did the writer use to tell the story? 1st   3rd
       How do you know?
       Is the point of view consistent throughout the story? Yes   No

4.   Circle the elements the writer used in the story:

"Dialogue" (characters talking to each other)

"Monologue" (character's thoughts)

Effective description of characters (you can visualize the character/understand the character's personality)

Effective (uses details) description of places (setting: time, place, mood)

Effective (uses details) description of things, objects, clothing (colors, exact numbers, names of flowers or candy bars or streets, names of TV shows or movies, smells, sounds, textures, tastes)

Symbolism

Flashbacks

Similes/metaphors

Internal conflict

External conflict

Name other elements the writer used:

5.   Go back over the list and make suggestions to the writer about where two elements can be added. (Where, for instance, can the writer use dialogue? More detailed descriptions?)

6.   Write a positive reaction to the story:

FIGURE 31–3 Three
Students' Paragraphs Using
Vocabulary from Reading

Student 1

He looked *covetously* at the body of a young woman in the pink chiffon dress sprawled on the pavement. *Overwrought* with lack of sleep, he moved with loose, *lethargical* movements, wishing he had a chance to lay as still as she did. She had been *bludgeoned* to death, and a large blood stain *emblazoned* her right shoulder. He looked around at the *pandemonium* the discovery of her body had caused. The police had erected a *barricade* to keep back the curious crowd. An old woman near the front began to *swoon* as they removed the lifeless young form.

Student 2

As he walked through the *vestibule* and out onto the lawn, the *mellifluous* smell of the ocean filled his nostrils. The *fluctuating* of the waves drew his attention to the beach. He noticed his friend, Sammy, near the lifeguard tower pestering the woman that walked by with his cheesy pick-up lines. Sammy wasn't the pick of the litter and was unbelievably clumsy. He always seemed to be *ostracized* by others because of his compulsive eating habits.

Student 3

The *mediocrity* of her insignificant life swept *mellifluously* over her weak body. That was how Shecher remembered herself; a naïve, dismal little girl, who morphed into a paranoid teenager. *Ostracized* most her life, she no longer minded being alone. She sat quietly on a bench, pushed her long dark hair out of her still very pale face. New York was quiet and warm, rather unusual. Shecher looked up at the sky. "Shecher," said a voice she recognized. She suddenly disdained the *inevitable* situation at hand. "Shecher, is that you?"

---

fiction. We discuss the time necessary to revise and rewrite to more accurately meet the requirements of the assignment and negotiate a due date for the final drafts.

It is important to realize that our students are still learning these words even though they've used them in a "final" draft. They are in the process of moving words from their reading to their writing vocabulary, and more practice will help them improve. Figure 31–3 shows three examples of paragraphs from student-written stories. In each paragraph, the student uses words from the lists in Figure 31–1.

CHOCOLATE FROSTING: READING THE STORIES ALOUD AND AWARDING A PRIZE

On the day the final drafts are due, students may read their stories to the class for extra credit, which amounts to two points. To read, the student must have the final draft ready to turn in. In my classes, extra credit is very rare and is connected to work already completed, not used to make up for skipped assignments. Students open their journals and write down the date and the word they taught the class. Then as each student reads his or her story, they listen for their word. When they hear it, they write the name of the student who used the word they taught. The student whose word is used the most wins! Usually I buy some supersize candy bars to give away. We check the list—the "winner" reads the list of students who used his or her word, they confirm their use of the word, and I award the prize.

After I've read and evaluated all the stories, I read some more of the stories aloud and post some of them on the bulletin board. Of course, I also keep copies of a few stories in my files so I have models to share next year.

The layers of this assignment take considerable time, but they accomplish the goal: multiple exposures to vocabulary words. Students complain that writing the story is difficult; wonderful—I want them to work hard. Students say the stories are fun; marvelous—I want them to realize that learning is a gratifying and enjoyable experience.

THE EXCITEMENT OF WORDS

Cathy Cirimele

"'The ride was exciting'. How can we expand this sentence into a descriptive paragraph that conveys the feeling of excitement? What words can we use to express that? Remember the phrase 'show, don't tell'? Would using the five senses help to describe the excitement of this ride?"

This is the way I begin teaching descriptive writing to my students every year. It doesn't matter what grade level I am instructing; all of my students—from regular ninth graders to advanced placement students—need to be reminded how powerful words can be. Without description, a story cannot be told.

Even though I know their teachers may have been instructing them year after year in the specifics of description and narration, my students seem to be blank slates when they enter my classroom and I first discuss these topics. I'm not sure *tabula rasa* is an accurate term for them. At any rate, whether I am truly trying to teach students about something they know nothing about, or I am simply jiggling some sluggish brain cells into recollection, I seem to have the most success with descriptive writing when I start with the basic approach of using sensory details.

PROCEDURE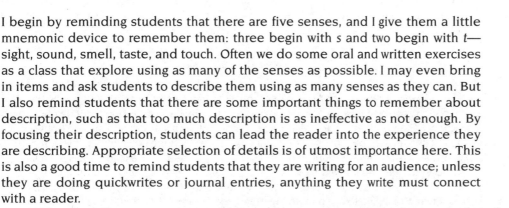

I begin by reminding students that there are five senses, and I give them a little mnemonic device to remember them: three begin with *s* and two begin with *t*— sight, sound, smell, taste, and touch. Often we do some oral and written exercises as a class that explore using as many of the senses as possible. I may even bring in items and ask students to describe them using as many senses as they can. But I also remind students that there are some important things to remember about description, such as that too much description is as ineffective as not enough. By focusing their description, students can lead the reader into the experience they are describing. Appropriate selection of details is of utmost importance here. This is also a good time to remind students that they are writing for an audience; unless they are doing quickwrites or journal entries, anything they write must connect with a reader.

Using specific sentences as writing prompts encourages students to take chances. After working as a class on some sample sentences, I usually give the class one to write on their own. The sentence I most often give them first is: *The ride was exciting*. I have collected photos that portray the idea of the sentence, and I show them to the class. These may come from newspapers, magazines, books, and personal photographs as well as other sources. The danger here is that the students often end up describing the photo instead of creating their own image.

The students have three to five minutes to quickwrite incorporating the sentence and using as much descriptive vocabulary as they can. This is the beginning of moving the sentence into what will become a paragraph. I want them to experiment and even exaggerate at this point, reminding them to use all five senses because it is a quickwrite. At the end of the quickwrite, I give them a few minutes to rewrite and revise it into a paragraph. Then I ask them to share their drafts with another student. During this sharing time, they discuss the strengths and weaknesses of their paragraphs and how their use of sensory detail provided images in their partner's mind. It doesn't seem to intimidate them as much if they have to share with only one other person whom they can choose. I encourage the students to give each other suggestions for improvement. Then they rewrite the paragraph. When they are finished, I ask them to underline all of the descriptive words and make a list, a cluster, or even a graph of what senses they are using. The format is up to them. This is a good way to get students to see that they often rely on sight description instead of employing other sensory details that might be more effective. Their homework assignment is to take the paragraph home and rewrite it as a final piece of writing.

The next day, I ask students to share their paragraph with small groups of four or five students. Each group then picks the paragraph that it thinks is most effective, and those paragraphs are read to the entire class. Because the students have each had a chance to revise and rework their writing, many of these paragraphs are good examples of descriptive writing. Figure 32–1 shows one student's paragraphs both before and after revision.

FIGURE 32–1 Student Writing

Quickwrite

The ride was exciting. It was loud and fast. Everyone was screaming and putting their hands up. As we climbed up higher and higher, I could feel my stomach turn. My hands began to sweat and I held the metal bar tighter. Then we started to go down and my stomach seemed to jump up into my mouth. My eyes were drying out from the wind blowing in them and my hair was blowing in my eyes. I wanted the ride to end. I thought I was going to be sick. I could hear everyone screaming loudly in front and behind me. Then it was over and I wanted to ride it again.

Final copy

As we climbed higher and higher, my stomach began to churn. My hands were sweating and I had trouble holding on to the hot metal bar I had clung to for safety and support. Finally we reached the top. Everyone started to scream and stick their hands up into the air, including me. As the roller coaster car plunged downwards, my stomach jumped into my dry, nervous mouth. I felt both nausea and excitement. I squinted through my hair which was beating me mercilessly. "Please hurry and end. Don't let me die," was all I could think of as we descended endlessly over the ocean. Then it was over. We jerked to a stop and my friend and I stared at each other in shock. "Let's go again!" I shouted. We eagerly hopped out of the car and ran unsteadily to the back of the line. It would be another hour before we could experience one minute of terror again.

CONCLUSION

I like this exercise and the impact it has on students for several reasons. It is an interesting and nonthreatening approach to beginning our study of writing, but it also teaches students that writing is a conscious activity that requires revision and work in order to choose words effectively. After all, writing should always encompass intensive word work through sharing, rewriting, and re-creating images that intrigue and connect with both the writer and the reader. It is what makes those of us who love writing continue to read and write on our own as well as attempt to convey that passion to the students we teach.

CURRICULUM-RELATED WORD BANKS: DEPOSITS THAT DRAW INTEREST

Kathleen Markovich

Before reading our first play of the school year, I ask students to brainstorm and list as many play- or drama-related words as they can. My students are seated in groups of four, and we use the small marbled composition books for language practice, quickwrites, literature journals, and reflections; we call them our journals. So out come the journals, and the oral brainstorming begins.

The purposes for this activity are many. The brainstorming and listing constitute our language practice for the day, and language practice is the way I begin my classes every day. We are activating our prior knowledge about plays and drama, and we are in groups, so we are sharing this knowledge with others. We are also creating a word bank—words we can use to discuss and write about the play as we read.

This time, after we share our lists and create a word bank, I plan to ask students to use the words to write sentences about drama. Some of my students' writing is still littered with comma splices and run-on sentences, so writing sentences and sharing them will give the students practice, reinforce the vocabulary, and give me a chance to assess and reteach "the sentence."

PROCEDURE

The following are the steps I follow to guide my students in the word bank activity:

1. At the overhead, I write *Drama/Play Words*.
2. Next, I write some examples: *actor, stage*.
3. Then I ask students to work in their groups to brainstorm and list 12 to 15 drama- or play-related words. As they work in groups, students usually start off calling out words to each other, but then they grow possessive of their ideas and start whispering their words and quietly writing lists.
4. When I sense the groups are finished, I call on individuals to contribute words to our word bank. I write them on the overhead, and the rest of the class copies words they don't already have in their journals. The list generated by one of my classes is shown in Figure 33–1.

script	makeup	audience	monologue
stage	intermission	character	protagonist
set	climax	music	downstage
costumes	curtain call	lines	director
storyline	playwright	narrator	critic
improvisation	Broadway	props	roles
lights	antagonist	technician	acts
conflict	scenes	backstage	applause

FIGURE 33–1 Student-Generated Bank of Play- or Drama-Related Words

1. After the *curtain call*, the actors took the stage to bow to the *audience*.
2. The *director* stood and bowed also, then the *playwright* took a bow.
3. Then the *lights* were dimmed, the *technicians* cleared the stage and put away the *props*, and the actors went *backstage* to take off their *costumes*.
4. The *actor* yelled at the *director* because during her *monologue*, the *prop* was not set in the proper position by the *techie*, the *lights* were not in the proper place, and her *costume* did not fit her *character* so the *audience* did not *applaud*.

FIGURE 33–2 Student-Generated Sentences

jury	judge	adjourned	evidence
witness	justice	defendant	prosecutor
witness stand	attorney	objection	bailiff
recess	verdict	gavel	victim
subpoena	suspect	plaintiff	sentence
appellate	oath	acquitted	testimony
jail	prison	overruled	

FIGURE 33–3 Student-Generated Bank of Court Words

5. After we generate the word bank, I ask students to take a few minutes and use 10 of the words in sentences. The maximum number of sentences they can write is three, and they have to underline their 10 words. Examples of student-generated sentences are shown in Figure 33–2.
6. Finally I call on 8 to 10 students to share their sentences. This gives me an opportunity to assess their sentence-writing skills, review one or two punctuation rules, and praise them for their progress in using a variety of structures and combining sentences to create longer, more mature sentences.

EXTENSIONS

The play we are about to read is *Twelve Angry Men*, by Reginald Rose (1956), so the next day, we brainstorm court-related words and write sentences using these words. The student-generated word bank is shown in Figure 33–3. If the play were Shakespearean, I would have students brainstorm Elizabethan words. Later in the year, when we began a poetry writing unit, we brainstormed words related to poetry.

CONCLUSION

The lesson about drama-related words gave drama students a chance to shine and share their knowledge; their group members appreciated their contributions. The lesson also gave me an opportunity to teach the correct spelling of *playwright* and to explain how a play is *wrought* in multiple dimensions, much like wrought iron.

As I stated, the lesson serves multiple purposes, such as language and vocabulary building, sentence practice, and activating prior knowledge. When we moved on to poetry, the word bank gave me a good assessment of what the students already knew about poetry and saved time because there were aspects, such as *simile* and *alliteration*, I did not have to reteach.

Language practice can be curriculum related and quite enjoyable. For the most part, learning about language draws interest from my students, and I find it gratifying to experience teaching and learning that is both productive and pleasurable.

REFERENCE

Rose, R. (1956). *Six television plays by Reginald Rose*. New York: International Famous Agency.

MONSTER SENTENCES

Lisa Twiford

Literature is the creative basis for many language arts lessons in my class. While reading the Stepping Stone Book Classics version of *Frankenstein*, by Mary Shelley and adapted by Larry Weinberg (1982), my students became fascinated with the ability to create a superhuman. I wanted them to incorporate this fascination into their writing, so I decided that we would become inventors of "monster sentences" to make our writing powerful.

PROCEDURE

To begin our lesson on creating "monster sentences," we first needed a skeleton on which to build our expanded sentences. I brought into class a Barbie-sized plastic skeleton to introduce the use of simple sentences as a "skeleton sentence." I had the students describe the skeleton. Their responses ranged from "It's plain" and "It's boring" to "It supports the body."

Next I asked questions about the skeleton: "Is it male or female?" "What color are its eyes or hair?" Naturally, the students guessed at the answers, but finally they admitted they didn't know because there wasn't enough information available. Then I explained how a skeleton is like a simple sentence: Both are needed for support; but when they are alone, both are boring and nondescript. To transform a plain skeleton into a unique human being, physical details must be added to the skeleton to form the body. With simple sentences, different parts of speech are used to transform them into longer, more interesting sentences. Like any good inventor, we practiced for a while, finding simple sentences in the story that could be used as *skeletons* for longer sentences. For instance, we liked the sentence: "Deep in the forest was a cave" (p. 49) as a skeleton.

Once we were able to recognize "skeleton sentences," we designed a graveyard where we could go, like Dr. Frankenstein, to "dig up" words to add to our sentences. In small groups, the students cut out gray, traditional-looking RIP tombstones. Each group was assigned a part of speech: they wrote the name of the part of speech with its definition at the top of the tombstone. Below the definitions, the groups listed interesting words for use in their writing. Figures 34–1 and 34–2 show sample tombstones: one for adjectives, one for nouns. The tombstones were stapled on a *Word Graveyard* on the wall. Throughout the month, additional appealing words were written on the appropriate tombstones.

During the discussion about how Dr. Frankenstein learned the secret for "putting life into a lifeless thing" (p. 10), my students decided that he must have

FIGURE 34–1 Adjective Tombstone

FIGURE 34–2 Noun Tombstone

devised a formula for creating the monster. We decided that we also needed to write a formula for creating our expanded monster sentences. Dr. Frankenstein knew what his perfect specimen would look like: "He was going to be big. Eight feet tall! And stronger than any man or woman on earth" (p. 11). Like Dr. Frankenstein, we also needed to know what a good monster sentence looked like. We decided that it had to be a long sentence because the creature in the book was over eight feet tall. The sentence must also include details that tell the how, why, when, what, and where; these details would add strength to sentences and make them powerful, like the monster. We used the book to find examples to fit our description:

"I wanted to do what God himself had done when he created people." (p. 10)
"It was I who had thought my creature would be beautiful." (p. 12)

Then we created some of our own examples and wrote them on a chart:

Skeleton sentence: I love to skateboard.
Monster Sentence: I love to do two different stances on my skateboard at home when I'm done with my homework.
Skeleton Sentence: I like to read Harry Potter.
Monster Sentence: I like to read the magical, interesting Harry Potter books whenever I have nothing to do.

With a clear vision of what a good monster sentence looks like, my students worked on writing interesting expanded sentences in their groups. Each group shared its creations and the class chose the best ones, which were then displayed on the overhead projector. Here are some examples:

The ugly green-faced monster wanted to make friends real bad with the villagers.
The lonely, miserable, sad monster killed the scared little boy because he was mad at Dr. Frankenstein.

The class discussed the order of words used in each sentence until a formula slowly emerged from the lively debate. Students observed: "You need several describing words to make the monster seem real"; "You need to use prepositions to tell where the action happened"; "The sentences are real long but more interesting." On a transparency, I wrote the "formula" and continually revised it until the class was satisfied with the final version.

Here are their steps for creating monster sentences:

1. Choose a "skeleton sentence."
2. Go to the *Word Graveyard* to gather parts of speech to use in making your "monster sentence" more interesting.
3. Create a "monster sentence" by using the monster formula:
   - Add an article to the beginning of the sentence.
   - Add one or two adjectives to describe the noun.
   - Use multisyllable verbs.
   - Use an adverb to tell more about the action.
   - Add a prepositional phrase to tell where the action is taking place.

After the whole class agreed on the formula, it was written on a chart and posted near the *Word Graveyard*. I made a copy of the formula for my students to keep in their binders and use as a reference for their home writing assignments.

CONCLUSION

Once the students finished this lesson, they loved to create longer, more interesting sentences in their writing. While students conferenced with their partners, it was common to hear them tell each other that they needed to use more monster sentences in their stories. As a teacher, I discovered that my experiment with turning my students into inventors was very successful. Our writing came alive, just like Dr. Frankenstein's monster!

REFERENCE

Shelly, M. (1982). *Frankenstein* (Adapted by L. Weinberg). New York: Bantam Books.

DON'T READ THIS; IT'S TABOO

Kathleen Markovich

"Snakes were not mentioned now, were not mentionable." (p. 48)
" 'Jack.' A taboo was evolving round that word too." (p. 127)

In William Golding's *Lord of the Flies* (1954), fear is the driving force behind taboo words. Early in the novel, when the boys fear the *beastie* that comes after them at night, *snake* is the taboo word. *Jack* becomes a taboo word later when Jack's tribe, wearing painted faces and howling till the "littluns" scream, raids the huts. My purposes for invoking the rule of taboo words are less dramatic: build vocabulary and develop an awareness of one's own style.

PROCEDURE

Sometime in the second quarter, once students are more aware of the writing process and my expectations, I write *Taboo Words* on the chalkboard, and then I write one or two—*good* and *bad* or *happy* and *sad*. I explain that in the next essay, these two words cannot appear in the final drafts because there are more precise words to use—better, but not necessarily longer, words. Sometimes people are not just *happy*; they're *jubilant, elated, amused, ecstatic*. Sometimes people are not *sad*; they're *troubled, regretful, miserable, sullen, melancholy*. "There is an abundance of accurate and specific words just waiting to be used, and it's about time you learned to use some of them," I explain.

In groups of four, which is how my desks are arranged, students brainstorm a list of words to use in place of the taboo words. Yes, published lists of adjectives or synonyms already exist in books such as *The Reading Teacher's Book of Lists* (Frye, Kress, & Fountoukidis, 2006), but I prefer asking my students to create their own lists. They can create lists that are just as long and precise as published ones, they take ownership of their list ("Our list is better than Period 4's"), the time invested in creating the list is time spent talking about vocabulary and word choice, and I think they will more readily consult their own list rather than a published one I hand out.

After allowing three or four minutes for brainstorming, I go to the overhead and start calling on students, and we create our list of alternate words. I record them on the transparency while the students copy them in their journals, where they can refer to them whenever they need to during the writing process. This step creates those wonderful moments when students argue over correct spelling and someone consults a dictionary, or the exact meaning is in question and someone looks it up. Handing out a published list might be easier and faster, but it's not teaching and learning. Teaching and learning are time-consuming and difficult, but worth every struggling moment.

As we proceed through the writing process of the next assignment, I remind students to remain alert: "Watch out for taboo words," I caution. Taboo words force students to pay attention to their word choices and give them a clear purpose and a definite task during peer response and editing. For example, an especially effective use for taboo words is replacing *said* in dialogue. Again, published lists of alternatives are readily available, but I still prefer student-generated lists. Some ideas for taboo words are: *said, thing, important, big, little, happy, sad, love, hate, good, bad, mad, go* (went), *very, lots*—any words you are tired of reading.

EXTENSIONS AND VARIATIONS

When we are writing descriptive essays or short fiction, I make generic words taboo, such as *tree, candy bar, car,* and *flowers. The flowers in the vase were beautiful and fragrant.* What does that sentence do for you? Do you see and smell the flowers? Did the writer help you "see" the scene? Now try this sentence: *The scent of the gardenias led her from the door to the bouquet.* Using the names of specific trees, candy bars, cars, and flowers helps the writer "show" and the reader "see," so we create lists using the specific words chart in Figure 35–1. "Trees" is one category—and students brainstorm specific trees for each letter of the alphabet: <u>a</u>pple, <u>b</u>irch, <u>c</u>amphor, <u>d</u>ogwood, and <u>e</u>lm. Flowers are <u>a</u>sters, <u>b</u>egonias, <u>c</u>amellias, <u>d</u>aisies, and <u>e</u>delweiss. Students consult these lists as they write, and the exercise forces them to become cognizant of the difference between general or vague words and specific word choices, such as *Camar̀o, Juicy Fruit, Cocker Spaniel,* and *magenta,* words that help writers "show" and readers "see."

Word walls can be used to record lists of words to use in place of lists of taboo words (to learn more about word walls, see the articles by Eileen Boland and Jared Kaiser in this book). My students keep their lists in their journals, which have the advantage of being portable—the journals go home with them. But word walls are effective banks for vocabulary lists, and I use them, too.

To help students differentiate among words that have different shades of the same meaning, use "Synonym Continuum," by Rebecca Wheeler in this book. Once students brainstorm a list of words to use instead of *sad,* for example, they can create a continuum of their synonyms. This continuum helps them choose the best words to use to relate the proper connotation in their own writing.

CONCLUSION

When John Steinbeck describes Lennie in *Of Mice and Men* (1937), his language is precise: "Behind him walked his opposite, a huge man, shapeless of face, with large, pale eyes, with wide, sloping shoulders; and he walked heavily, dragging his feet a little, the way a bear drags his paws" (p. 2). Just as our students need to be aware of Steinbeck's word choices, they need to be aware of their own, not perhaps when they are drafting essays, but when they are revising and responding to the writing of their peers. Taboo words help students become aware of style and the power of precise language.

REFERENCES

Fry, E., Kress, J., & Fountoukidis, D. (2006). *The reading teacher's book of lists.* (5th ed.) Upper Saddle River, NJ: Merrill/Prentice Hall.

Golding, W. (1954). *Lord of the flies.* New York: Putnam.

Name_____

Date_____Period_____

SPECIFIC NAMES/WORDS/NOUNS

List the four general categories across the top, then fill in a specific name/word/noun for each letter of the alphabet for each category.

A				
B				
C				
D				
E				
F				
G				
H				
I				
J				
K				
L				
M				
N				
O				
P				
Q				
R				
S				
T				
U				
V				
W				
X				
Y				
Z				

FIGURE 35–1   Specific Word Chart

Investigating Word Origins

Students who know about root words and word histories can use their knowledge to unlock the meaning of hundreds of unfamiliar words. Strategies they might use include *morphology*, or the study of roots and their derivatives; *etymology*, or the study of word origins; and *lexicology*, or the study of word origins as it relates to the lexicographers or the compilers of dictionaries.

Bear, Invernizzi, Templeton, and Johnston (2004) suggest that readers benefit from the study of morphology. Through their studies they have found that "beginning with known words and then expanding to include unknown words, having awareness of the spelling–meaning connection will not only help students fine tune their spelling ability, but also help expand their vocabulary" (p. 252). Diane Highbaugh, Kathleen Markovich, and Cathy Blanchfield ("Word Tree Posters") all share activities that help students add prefixes and suffixes to base words and create new words related in meaning.

Because there are so many words to learn and most learning occurs while students read, it is necessary to help students develop the "cognitive disposition toward words . . . called 'word consciousness'" (Graves & Watts-Taffe, 1992, p. 145). Tompkins (2006) concurs by explaining that when students discover and trace the development of the English language "they appreciate the relationships among words and their meanings" (p. 205). Gail Tompkins and Laurie Goodman's lessons in this chapter present enjoyable activities that assist students with learning etymologies and promote word consciousness.

Word consciousness is also encouraged as students learn how lexicographers choose words for new editions of dictionaries. Malisa Ervin and Cathy Blanchfield ("From Slang to Dictionary Entry: A Word Study Project") have written activities that help students understand lexicology and even participate in predicting new entries for the dictionary.

The more students investigate words and their derivatives and origins, the more they will recognize and understand new words in their own reading.

REFERENCES

Bear, D. R., Invernizzi, M., Templeton, S., & Johnston, F. (2004). *Words their way*: *Word study for phonics, vocabulary, and spelling instruction* (3rd ed.). Upper Saddle River, NJ: Merrill/Prentice Hall.

Graves, M. F., & Watts-Taffe, S. M. (1992). The place of word consciousness in a research-based vocabulary program. In A. E. Farstrup, & S. J. Samuels (Eds.), *What research has to say about reading instruction* (2nd ed., pp. 140–165). Newark, DE: International Reading Association.

Tompkins, G. E. (2006). *Literacy for the 21st century*: *A balanced approach* (4th ed.). Upper Saddle River, NJ: Merrill/Prentice Hall.

WHERE IN THE WORLD?

Gail Tompkins

English is a world language. English speakers have enriched the language by borrowing words from just about every language in the world, and today we use these "world" words every day (Tompkins & Yaden, 1986). The origin of some food words is easy to guess: *Pizza* and *spaghetti* are Italian, as you know, but so are *broccoli* and *cantaloupe*. Others are trickier: *yogurt* is Turkish, *potato* is Spanish, *coconut* is Portuguese, *pretzel* is German, and *pickle* is Dutch. In addition to food words, English has borrowed words related to every aspect of life: *kindergarten* is German, *hallelujah* is Hebrew, *robot* is Czechoslovakian, *hurricane* is Spanish, *mathematics* is Greek, *alcohol* is Arabic, *safari* is from an African language, *jungle* is Hindi, *tycoon* is Chinese, and *chagrin* is French.

Words from other languages have entered English throughout the history of the language. The Vikings, who invaded England before the first millennium, contributed *awkward*, *sleuth*, *kindle*, *whirl*, and many other common words. William the Conqueror and the French who ruled England from 1066 to approximately 1300 contributed other words, especially military words and words related to the arts. Latin and Greek words entered English during the Renaissance, and more than half of our words today have Latin and Greek word parts. Still other words entered English through the English explorers who traveled the world in the 17th and 18th centuries. *Kangaroo*, for example, is an Australian word that means "I don't know." According to legend, an English explorer asked his aboriginal guide about the unusual animal, and the guide answered "kangaroo," which meant "I don't know" in his language.

PROCEDURE

The focus of this lesson is to increase students' awareness of the richness of the English language by exploring how words enter English and how a word's etymology or history helps to explain its meaning and spelling. Learning about word histories is especially important for English learners who are often baffled by multiple meanings of words and seemingly bizarre English spelling patterns (Bear, Templeton, Helman, & Baren, 2003). Most words that have entered English from Arabic, for example, begin with *al*, which in Arabic is similar to our article *the*; examples include *alcohol*, *algebra*, *alfalfa*, *Allah*, and *alkali*. Words with *ch* are interesting, too. Those where the *ch* is pronounced /ch/, as in *charcoal*, are English. But when *ch* is pronounced /sh/ as in *chauffeur*, the words are French, and when *ch* is pronounced /k/ as in *chaos* and *chorus*, the words are Greek.

Teachers begin by posting a large world map in the classroom and, during the school year, they assist the students in making and adding small word cards to the country representing the language the word came from or the geographic area where the word was first used. On each card, students write the word, the language, and the original meaning.

Millennium is an interesting example.

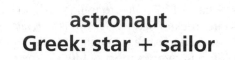

> # Millennium
> ## Latin: thousand years

The word *millennium* is a Latin word meaning "thousand, years"; *mille* means "thousand," and *enn* means "years." The Latin word part meaning years has two forms—*ann* and *enn*. Other *ann/enn* words include *annual, anniversary, bicentennial perennial,* and *sesquicentennial.*

Astronaut is an interesting Greek word:

> # astronaut
> ## Greek: star + sailor

Astronaut means "sailor to the stars," and the two word parts are *astro* (or "star") and *naut* (or "sailor"). It is interesting to compare the word *astronaut* to *cosmonaut,* the Russian equivalent meaning "sailor to the universe," which is also a Greek word.

Another fascinating word is *umbrella*:

> # umbrella
> ## Italian: shade

Umbrella comes from the Italian word for "shade" and literally means "a little bit of shade." Perhaps *umbrellas* were first used to protect people from the sun, not from the rain.

Students can check the etymology or word history of any words they are studying, but those that do not conform to English phonic rules or that look "foreign" are often the most interesting. High school- and college-level dictionaries provide etymological information, usually bracketed at the beginning or end of the entry. Here is the etymological information for *millennium, astronaut,* and *umbrella*:

> *Millennium* [L *mille* thousand + years]
> *astronaut* [Gr *astro,* star + *naut,* sailor <*naus,* ship]
> *umbrella* [Ital. dim. of *ombra,* shade]

Teachers looking for some interesting words to investigate can consult Figure 36–1, which presents a list of "world" words. These words came into English from a variety of languages, and the etymological information is easy to understand.

FIGURE 36–1 Words from around the World

aardvark	gymnast	revive
abode	hallelujah	revolution
adversary	hamburger	reward
alphabet	hammock	rhapsody
America	hibachi	riffraff
amoeba	hippopotamus	robot
assassin	hue	rodeo
balcony	hurricane	salary
ballot	hydrant	sarcastic
barbecue	jubilee	savory
bazaar	kayak	schmuck
bivouac	khaki	scold
bizarre	kimono	serendipity
bonanza	kiosk	shampoo
bonus	kudos	siesta
bungalow	labyrinth	slogan
bureau	levee	skirt
cache	mosquito	skunk
calorie	motto	solo
canoe	mukluk	spider
canyon	mumbo jumbo	stampede
capillary	music	suede
carnivorous	mustang	suicide
caustic	null	superficial
chameleon	nutrition	tattoo
chaparral	nuzzle	tawdry
chemistry	opossum	teepee
chic	opulent	thermometer
chocolate	oral	thug
chutzpah	ouch	titantic
circuit	outlaw	tornado
cobra	pajamas	tundra
coyote	panache	typhoon
crocodile	paprika	ugly
cul-de-sac	paradox	utopia
curry	parka	vagabond
czar	pastrami	vampire
delicatessen	peccadillo	vaudeville
dexterity	pentagon	venom
enemy	periscope	villian
energy	phenomenon	wampum
epidemic	pique	wednesday
extravaganza	piranha	woman
fickle	porcupine	yankee
fragile	prairie	yoga
frankfurter	privy	zenith
frequent	protégé	zero
frolic	quench	
gopher	rancor	

Some good books have been written about word histories. The entries in these books provide more information than is possible in a brief dictionary etymology. My favorite ones are:

Fine, E. H. (2004). *Cryptomania!: Teleporting into Greek and Latin with the Crypto Kids.* Berkeley, CA: Tricycle.

Funk, W. (1992). *Word origins: An exploration and history of words and language.* New York: Wings Press.

Funk, C. E. (2002). A *hog on ice and other curious expressions*. New York: HarperCollins.

Funk, C. E. (2002). *Horsefeathers and other curious words*. New York: HarperCollins.

Lederer, R. (1990). *The play of words*. New York: Pocket Books.

The Merriam-Webster new book of word histories. (1995). Springfield, MA: Merriam-Webster.

Terban, M. (1988). *Guppies in tuxedos: Funny eponyms*. New York: Clarion.

Word histories and mysteries: From abracadabra to Zeus. (2004). Boston: Houghton Mifflin.

AMERICAN ENGLISH WORDS

Some English words are American originals. Words such as *canoe*, *skunk*, and *raccoon* were Native American words that were Anglicized by the English-speaking colonists, and others were invented by the colonists. *Yankee*, for example, was coined in the Dutch colony of New Amsterdam. Linguists have speculated that *Yankee* began as the Dutch form of *Johnny* to refer to the English colonists of New England.

Other words have been coined by Americans throughout the history of the United States. *Frontier*, *prairie*, *Underground Railroad*, *immigrant*, and *cowboy* are older examples. More recent examples are UFO, *workaholic*, *filibuster*, *cafeteria*, and *hijack*, and undoubtedly words made in America will continue to enrich the English language. For more information about these and other American English words, check Metcalf and Barnhart's *America in So Many Words: Words That Have Shaped America* (1997).

Still other words have entered English from Mexico. The most familiar are Mexican food words such as *chocolate*, *chili*, *taco*, *tomato*, and *tortilla*. Other Mexican Spanish words associated with cowboys and the settlement of the southwestern states include *ranch*, *coyote*, *lasso*, *mustang*, *canyon*, *corral*, and *palomino*. Teachers who teach American history might want to post a map of the United States and add American English words to the map as part of the study of American history.

CONCLUSION

In addition to familiarizing students with the locations of countries and other geographic concepts, this activity clarifies students' confusions about many words. Also, it heightens students' interest in words and the stories about how words enter English.

REFERENCES

Bear, D. R., Templeton, S., Helman, L. A., & Baren, T. (2003). Orthographic development and learning to read in different languages. In G. G. Garcia (Ed.), *English learners: Reaching the highest level of English literacy* (pp. 71–95). Newark, DE: International Reading Association.

Metcalf, A., & Barnhart, D. K. (1997). *America in so many words: Words that have shaped America*. Boston: Houghton Mifflin.

Tompkins, G. E., & Yaden, D. B., Jr. (1986). *Answering students' questions about words*. Urbana, IL: National Council of Teachers of English.

FROM SLANG TO DICTIONARY ENTRY: A WORD STUDY PROJECT

Cathy Blanchfield

I love words. I love to hear stories about words. I love to read about how various cultures created and changed words to express their society. What I want to instill most in my students is this love of words, but it's a hard sell!

I came to realize how hard a sell this was a few years ago with a particularly nonresponsive group of seniors. Throughout the first quarter, we related words to history, to literature, and to stories from British culture. They politely listened and completed the activities, but they were not interested. In response, my last attempt to pull them into the "word lover circle" was an activity I developed to study how modern words are added to the dictionary. I decided that it was time for students to research and share. The result was that many came to see how we *can* enjoy our language together.

Now I begin each year with a word research project. We always enjoy the search as well as the presentation. This activity serves as a focal point for further vocabulary study throughout the year. Although the students may not "love" words, they now are intrigued by the coining of new words and are interested in possible further study.

PROCEDURE

I begin the project by explaining to the students how our language reflects our culture. We talk about how the dictionary is not a stagnant work but is dynamically undergoing additions and changes as our culture changes. I then introduce the many ways words are added to our dictionary. Some words are borrowed from another language; some are compounds. Some come from mythology and some from brand names. We add slang, create new concept words, clip some words for ease of speaking, and coin words as we need new expressions. I then hand out the directions for their word study project, as shown in Figure 37–1.

I ask each group to decide on a theme for their search. Students choose such themes as *teen culture*, *the environment*, and *merchandizing*. This theme provides the focus for their search as well as a structure for their presentation. The first night they are charged with finding reading material on this theme. They go to the library, find encyclopedias at home, log on to the Internet, and buy magazines. If their theme is *teen culture*, they may bring in a magazine published for teens; if their theme is *the environment*, they may run an Internet search for environmental issues and print one or two articles. This provides a "bank" of thematic words to find in the dictionary or other word origin resource.

FIGURE 37–1 Word Study Assignment

Word Study

Lexicographers list a variety of requirements that words must meet in order to be added to the dictionary. *Usage by the general population* and *staying power* are just two such requirements. It is always interesting to note how words have been added in the past, as well as to guess what words might make it into the next dictionary. Use all of the resources available to prepare a presentation for the class. Your group must work together to both prepare and present your information.

Before you make your collection, you must decide on a theme. Then all of the words you collect will relate to that theme. Sample themes are: environment, education, health, business, merchandizing, and space exploration.

Your presentation must include:

- examples of borrowed words from one language (Chinese, German, many others—find them in list form in the dictionary)

- examples of compounds (*briefcase* from the need for a *case* to carry *briefs* or written documents)

- examples of words that were coined from names (*Levis*) or brand names (*Coke*)

- examples of words that came from mythology (*atlas* from the Greek god who held up the world)

- examples of words that came from acronyms (*AIDS*)

- examples of portmanteau words (*brunch* from *breakfast* and *lunch*)

- examples of words that have been clipped (*math* for *mathematics*)

- at least one word with the story behind the word (*red herring*)

- examples of words that have been added to the dictionary in the past 10 years (*cell phone*)

- examples of slang that have been added to our dictionary as real words (*ain't*)

- examples of idiomatic expressions (*go fly a kite*!)

- examples of slang you think will be added in the next 10 years (your choice)

Try to make this interesting and informative for your classmates. They will need to take notes and enjoy your presentation. You must have both audio and visual portions in your presentation. A visual may be a poster, a VCR tape, or a PowerPoint presentation. Your audio may be included with the video (as on a VCR), a skit, a narration, or a talk. Your score will be based on the creativity of both your visuals and your talk. Everyone participates!

I discuss the many resources for research in our room. To begin, their literature books have some words listed. Also, the dictionary we use is a wonderful resource. In addition, I have collected a number of books for students to consult; Figure 37–2 is an annotated list of the resources I use. It is in no way exhaustive, but rather a good library for word research. Figure 37–3 lists a few useful websites for word study; students were constantly on the computers researching these sites.

While one or two students are reading the articles and collecting words to look up, others are reading the Panati books to find "stories behind the words" or the slang dictionaries to find words that fit their theme. Still others are seated at the class computers logging on to a variety of websites. All are busy. The discussions are intellectual and informative, as concerned students put together their collections of words for each assigned category (e.g., *borrowed words, words coined from names, acronyms,* and *slang*).

Fry, E. B., Kress, J. E., & Fountoukidis, D. L. (1993). *The reading teacher's book of lists* (3rd ed.). West Nyack, NY: Prentice Hall.

A collection of 150 word lists ranging from phonetic word groups to enrichment and discovery activity lists. This book includes an extensive listing of word origins grouped according to origin (e.g., acronyms and intializations, words borrowed from names, and words originating from mythology).

Panati, C. (1984). *Panati's browser's book of beginnings.* Boston: Houghton Mifflin.

The story behind hundreds of words arranged by topic (e.g., detailed stories are easy to understand and follow).

Panati, C. (1987). *Panati's extraordinary origins of everyday things.* New York: Harper & Row.

Much like his first book, this collection is truly a list of "ordinary" things. These stories are arranged by where or when we might find the words (i.e., "In the bathroom" or "By custom"). Another great collection of easy-to-follow stories.

Seifert, B., & Seifert, M. (1973). *Dictionary of local lingo.* Boston: Houghton Mifflin.

A book of slang and informal words and phrases. Easy to read and use.

Shipley, J. T. (1945). *Dictionary of word origins.* New York: Dorset Press.

A collection of word origins arranged alphabetically by the word. Many cross-references are included. High school and above reading level.

Terban, M. (1996). *Dictionary of idioms.* New York: Scholastic.

A wide variety of entries arranged by the first word of the idiom. Each entry gives not only the meaning of the phrase but also the story behind the idiom.

Thorndike, E. L., & Barnhart, C. L. (1988). *Scott, Foresman advanced dictionary.* Glenview, IL: Scott, Foresman.

This dictionary lists common words borrowed from other languages grouped according to the language of origin. It also lists some coined words and gives limited stories behind a few words.

FIGURE 37–2 An Annotated Bibliography of Reference Books

www.dictionary.reference.com

www.takeourword.com

www.wordorigins.org

www.acronymfinder.com

www.ask.com

www.etymonline.com

www.libraryspot.com

www.worldwodewords.org

www.wordwizard.com

FIGURE 37–3 Etymology and Word Study Websites

FIGURE 37–4 Word Origin Poster with Partial Enlargement

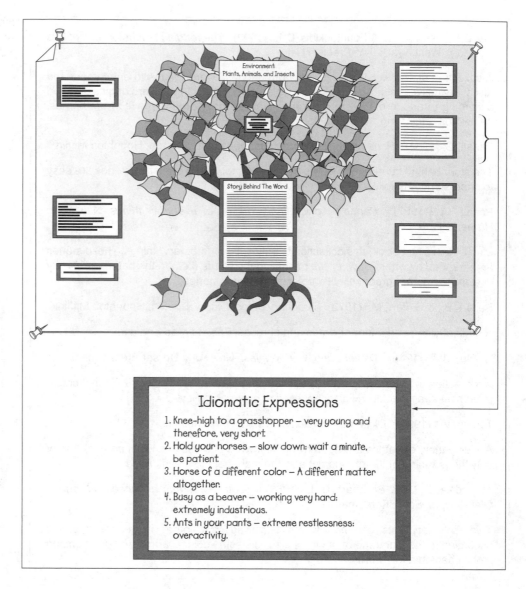

CONCLUSION

I am always awed by the creativity of my students. At least two groups in each class created a PowerPoint presentation. Students provided the narration while they clicked through screen after screen of new words. One group created a videotape of themselves sitting in a restaurant ordering foods from different countries. Their "menus" were organized by country, presenting the variety of *borrowed* food names. Other groups performed skits where they cleverly used and explained the meaning of a variety of words belonging to their theme. Many groups made posters that became the wall decorations (see Figure 37–4). Students walk into the class and read each other's posters before sitting in their seats.

The result is an attitude of appreciation for words and their additions to the dictionary. We will continue to enjoy words, use the dictionary, and "collect" categories of words throughout the year. My students and I have begun the *Word Appreciation Club.*

BACK TO OUR WORD ROOTS

Diane Highbaugh

Each of our families has its own wealth of stories that connect us to the past, provide a foundation to the present, and tether us to the future. We share anecdotes and favorite memories when relatives are together. We learn of the resolve, accomplishments, pain, and joys of preceding generations. Some of these stories become part of a collective identity, and others fade and are forgotten. These accounts anchor us and become part of our own identity. As we live, work, and discover life, we add our own stories to the files of the ancestral archive, so the family "story" is always changing. Understanding the story of our family helps us know who we are today. These stories root us in our present day.

Words in our language connect us to another heritage. Word roots are the stories of our language, and they help us discover how our language is embedded with meaning. Word roots connect us to sophisticated cultures with complex ideas, art, architecture, and spirituality of preceding generations that have had systematic methods of communicating. An awareness of the identity of these word parts helps us to understand the identity of the individual word. Word roots continue in the present and into the future by becoming parts of new words. The stories of the past continue and are embedded into the language of the future. It is important to know where we come from and where our language originates. This is why I promote the study of Greek word roots.

PROCEDURE

I have my students make word webs to study words made from Greek roots, and then students compile the word web papers to make books. These are the steps I use:

1. Divide the class into groups of four to six students.
2. Pass out a Greek word root list. *The Reading Teachers Book of Lists* (Fry, Kress, & Fountoukidis, 2006) is an excellent source for this hand-out.
3. Ask each student to choose two word roots to work with that are different from those chosen by the other people in the group.
4. Direct the students to use dictionaries or other resources to find four words that contain their chosen word root.
5. Have students sketch a rough draft word web for each word. On an 8.5 × 5.5-inch sheet of paper, students place the word root with its meaning in the middle ellipse. A sample word web is provided in Figure 38–1.
6. Direct the students to complete the outer rays of the web with related words and their meanings.

FIGURE 38–1 A
Completed Student Word
Web

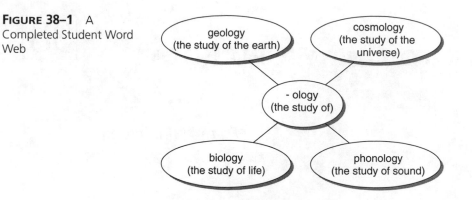

7. Suggest that students make small pictures around each ray to illustrate the word's meaning.
8. Ask students to share their rough drafts with a peer for editing before they complete their final drafts.
9. Compile the individual pages into a group book.

CONCLUSION

Each time I complete this activity, students have a better understanding of our language and its rich beginnings. In addition, students enjoy the connection to the ancient Greeks that our language provides.

REFERENCES

Fry, E., Kress, J., & Fountoukidis, D. (2006). *The reading teacher's book of lists.* (5th ed.) West Nyack, NY: Prentice Hall.

39

START YOUR DAY WITH VOCABULARY: IT'S LOW IN FAT AND HIGH IN FIBER

Kathleen Markovich

I teach 95-minute classes that rotate on an odd-even block (periods 1, 3, 5, and 7 one day; periods 2, 4, 6, and 8 the next day), and I start my classes with language practice, which alternates between sentence correction and vocabulary every 2 to 3 weeks. The vocabulary lessons, I thought, would be easy and quick ways to address the low scores that show up every time our standardized test scores are distributed, and they would add a little variety to our diet. The vocabulary lesson design is easy, but sometimes we spend 25 to 30 minutes discussing words before I check the time, so "quick" is not always an accurate descriptor. However, the time is well spent, and our students often reveal extensive vocabularies and a knowledge of language we are otherwise unaware of.

The lesson design is this: I provide a root or affix and the students generate a list of examples. We brainstorm, list, and discuss the words. My goal is to provide students with experience with specific roots and affixes that will help them to work with word choices when they compose and to recognize or figure out more words when they read and when they take standardized tests.

My sources for lists are a little paperback I found at Barnes & Noble: *Instant Vocabulary* (Ehrlich, 1968). Lists are also available in *The Reading Teacher's Book of Lists* (Fry, Kress, & Fountoukidis, 1993) and *Words, Words, Words: Teaching Vocabulary in Grades 4–12* (Allen, 1999). *Instant Vocabulary* also provides examples, definitions, word analysis, and practical exercises.

PROCEDURE

I follow these steps in teaching the vocabulary lesson on the suffix "al."

1. On the overhead, I write AL—*suffix—adjective meaning "relating to."*
2. Next, I write a couple of examples: *intellectual, spiritual.*
3. Using the names of students in the class, I create sentences to demonstrate the kind of words we're looking for. "Justin is an *intellectual* student who likes reading about Golding's ideas in *Lord of the Flies.*" "Erin is more *spiritual* than most; after all, she taught us about tarot cards."
4. Then I ask students, who are seated in groups of four, to work together to brainstorm 15 examples of AL words that fit the description and to write their lists in their journals. During the 3 to 5 minutes students are brainstorming, I hear snippets of student talk: "That isn't a real word. I'm gonna look it up." "Oh, that's a good one. How do you spell it?" "You better not use MY word!" "Shh! The other group is stealing our words." They're arguing about vocabulary words, consulting dictionaries, and protecting THEIR

FIGURE 39–1 Students'
Generated List

List of AL words			
personal	facial	skeptical	fatal
rational	physical	musical	criminal
international	neutral	emotional	cultural
eternal	verbal	herbal	dysfunctional
chemical	visual	sentimental	factual
educational	suicidal	sexual	natural

words. They are engaged, some are excited, and most are having fun—with words! I smile quietly.

5. Next, I call on individuals to contribute one AL word to our class list—I write the words on the overhead as students add the words they don't already have to the lists in their journals. The list generated by one of my classes is shown in Figure 39–1.

TEACHABLE MOMENTS

The act of listing creates wonderful "teachable moments." The word *interval*, for instance, is not an adjective; it doesn't fit the pattern—*face* to *facial*, *emotion* to *emotional*. AL thus is not a suffix in *interval*. Some words, such as *physical*, *musical*, and *criminal*, are nouns and adjectives; they have multiple meanings and provide the perfect opportunity to teach about that particular subtest of standardized tests. A person can be *physical*, take a *physical*, and study *physical* science. Sometimes, I can't spell the word (Is it *likable* or *likeable*?), or the student adding the word to the list spells the word incorrectly (*megabite*). For this lesson, two students have dictionaries and the responsibility of checking spelling, parts of speech, and definitions. Students challenge each other concerning definitions or usage, and I let the students defend their words.

The word *furious* gave me an opportunity to teach mythology—the furies, the avengers; it was a genuine and natural occasion to teach the state standard regarding words derived from mythology. *Expository* led to a lesson about writing and modes of discourse and reading and text patterns. The word *crucible* didn't fit the *able–ible* pattern, but it prompted a rant about the play, Arthur Miller, the Salem witch trials, and McCarthyism. My students are so lucky!

Our class list of OUS words contains 37 words because the students didn't want to stop. Their list is impressive: *tedious, precocious, zealous, blasphemous*. I was not aware they knew these words; I learned they were smarter than I thought, and that I could expect and demand more from them. My students are so lucky!

WARNING

Students will contribute questionable or risky words, such as *sexual, bisexual, homosexual, heterosexual, transexual*. I have taught for many years, and I don't fluster easily. As long as the word is a word and is not offensive, I nonchalantly add it to the list, using my matter-of-fact attitude to quell the giggles. If you are not comfortable with certain words, don't allow them. Do what makes you feel comfortable, and please don't risk your job over a vocabulary lesson.

EXTENSIONS AND VARIATIONS

For the next day, select 20 of the words for a word sort. If the list is adjectives, sort them by *person*, *place*, and *thing* for the type of noun they modify. Sort the words that have multiple meanings, or just hand out the words and let the students create categories and sort the words themselves. The purpose is to focus on word study and examine words, their meanings, and how they function in our language.

Change the parts of speech: Turn adjectives into adverbs or nouns or verbs—*natural* to *naturally* to *nature*; *outrage* to *outrageous* to *outrageously*; *excite* to *excitement* to *excited* to *excitedly*. I ask students, seated in groups of four, to work together to generate as many forms of the word as possible and to write the part of speech, if they can, in parentheses next to the words in their lists. Students will see how affixes change parts of speech and how they can use affixes to make educated guesses in the vocabulary subtests of multiple-choice tests.

CONCLUSION

Using vocabulary as part of language practice offers variety, a change of pace from the usual sentence corrections. Using vocabulary focuses on a very real need: Our students need vocabulary work to help them improve their reading comprehension. Student input during these lessons helped me realize how much my students already know about words and how extensive their vocabularies already are: test results truly show just one piece of the picture. As a bonus, vocabulary work as a part of language practice is often enjoyable, and students discover that vocabulary work and learning can be gratifying experiences.

REFERENCES

Allen, J. (1999). *Words, words, words: Teaching vocabulary in grades 4–12*. York, ME: Stenhouse.

Ehrlich, I. (1968). *Instant vocabulary*. New York: Simon & Schuster.

Fry, E., Kress, J., & Fountoukidis, D. (2006). *The reading teacher's book of lists*. (5th ed.) West Nyack, NY: Prentice Hall.

40

WORD TREE POSTERS

Cathy Blanchfield

The room is a forest of trees. There are pine trees, apple trees, oak trees, and ash trees; tall trees, short trees, squatty trees, and thin trees. They spill out into the hall, on doors, on movable dividers, on the walls. It's only the first of September, and there is already no empty display area. But wait! The "bark" of the trees is created with words. What kind of words? What are these growths?

After the California Department of Education published the *Reading/Language Arts Framework for California Public Schools* (1999), I knew that I needed to develop many more lessons on vocabulary and the origin of words. Up through 1998, my seventh and eighth graders received a lesson here and there about Greek and Latin roots, but no in-depth study of word origins and the development of our English language. I wanted to begin the year with an activity that we could build upon later. Although most of the students had been exposed to some Greek and Latin roots, to ensure that all students had the same background knowledge, I decided that they needed a study of the most common roots.

As a first-week activity, I now ask my students to make a word tree. They work with partners or triads to create their tree. Each tree begins with a root. I assign these roots so that we cover many of the common Greek and Latin roots. The root and its meaning are at the base of the tree. A list of the roots that I use is shown on the student activity direction page in Figure 40–1. Each group receives a piece of 12 × 18-inch art paper for this project. Each branch is dedicated to a word that contains the assigned root. Students brainstorm words they know that contain the roots. They try to make new words by adding prefixes and suffixes. Because they can find derivatives with suffixes in the dictionary, I do not give them a list. However, I do remind them of many common prefixes to aid their dictionary search. On each branch, the students write a definition of their new word, using the meaning of the root. For example, if the students are working with the root *rupt*, which means "to break," then the definition for *interrupt* is to break into a conversation.

This activity works well with students of all ability levels. As a way of scaffolding with my English language learners, I complete one word tree with the class before asking individuals to complete their own posters. Students not only enjoy the creation of their tree, but also develop an awareness of roots and a knowledge of some of the major building blocks of our language.

FIGURE 40–1 Student
Word Tree Directions

Word Tree Activity

Procedure:

- Select a root.
- Share with each other as many forms of this root as possible.
- Use the dictionary and the suffixes and prefixes that you know to try to find new words that you didn't think of.
- Write the words and a brief definition for each, using the meaning of the root in your definitions.
- Draw an outline of a tree.
- Write the root at the base of the tree and each new word and its definition on individual branches.

Possible high-frequency roots:

spec (Latin—see)	vid (Latin—see)
port (Latin—carry)	fac (Latin—make, do)
cred (Latin—believe)	ped (Latin—foot)
graph (Greek—write)	gram (Greek—letter, write)
man (Latin—hand)	therm (Greek—heat)
photo (Greek—light)	loc (Latin—place)
rupt (Latin—break)	phon (Greek—sound)
script (Latin—write)	mot (Latin—move)
tract (Latin—pull, drag)	cycl (Greek—circle, ring)
dic (Latin—speak)	aud (Latin—hear)

Try these prefixes (or any other that you remember from last year):

inter-	super-	counter-	ex-
intra-	fore-	post-	pro-
co-	com-	sub-	pre-
con-	anti-	de-	im-
in-	dis-	il-	ir-
un-	mis-	non-	re-

PROCEDURE

I read about word trees in *Words Their Way* (Bear, Invernizzi, Templeton, & Johnston, 2000) and adapted the idea for my classroom. I ask students to do the following:

1. Select a root.
2. Share with each other as many word forms of this root as possible.
3. Use the dictionary and the suffixes and prefixes that you know to find new words that you didn't think of.
4. Write the words and a brief definition for each using the meaning of the root in your definitions.
5. Draw an outline of a tree.
6. Write the root at the base of the tree and each new word and its definition on individual branches.

A tree for *dic*, a Latin root meaning "to speak," made by two of my students is shown in Figure 40–2. The words added to the tree were:

contradict: to speak against someone or something
predict: to speak what will happen before it does

FIGURE 40–2 Student
Word Tree

predicate: the part of a sentence expressing what is spoken about the
subject (usually containing the verb)
dictionary: a reference book containing all aspects of spoken language
dictum: an important spoken statement
dictator: one who speaks to rule many
dictate: to speak something for someone else to write
diction: how correctly one speaks

CONCLUSION

Many of these posters remain in the classroom and hall until Christmas. I notice students reading them often. As they wait to go into class, as they walk together through the halls, and as they sharpen their pencils, the posters are there for them to read. I am always amazed to see adolescents sharing a poster even after many months of seeing it in the hall. The forest remains alive for months after the initial assignment.

REFERENCES

Bear D., Invernizzi, M., Templeton, S., & Johnston, F. (2004). *Words their way* (3rd ed.). Upper Saddle River, NJ: Prentice Hall.

California State Board of Education. (1999). *Reading/language arts framework for California public schools*. Sacramento: California Department of Education.

41

LINKING THE PAST WITH THE PRESENT: MODERNIZING WORDS

Laurie Goodman

Teaching an eighth-grade language arts/history block is a perfect opportunity to discuss with students how our language and vocabulary have changed over the course of our country's history. My students are continuously encountering words with which they feel no connection. It is hard for today's students to believe there was life before computers and television, let alone connect with items from the past that performed similar functions to items in our world today.

Creating a "Time Warp" brochure that links the vocabulary of the past with the items that provide the same function in today's world is one way that students can increase their understanding of American history, their vocabulary knowledge, and the connection we have with days gone by. We start with Colonial America in history and work our way through Reconstruction. A sample list of words from the book *Pink and Say* (Polacco, 1994), a story we use during our Civil War Unit, included: *kit, marauders, vittles, winderlight, quartered, riding-drag, spectacles, buckboard, stockade, smote, knotted, hemp,* and *mustered.* As we encounter antiquated words, we decide if there is a word that represents the modern equivalent of the antiquated word. After we have generated our list from the history unit or the piece of literature that we are studying, we use the following activity to increase our understanding of the words.

PROCEDURE

My instructions to the students are as follows:

1. Determine the meaning of the old word as it is used in the unit of study or the piece of literature:
   a. Copy the sentence or passage as it appears with the word in it.
   b. Paraphrase the sentence or passage into your own words.
   c. Check for a dictionary definition of the word and compare that with the way the word is used in context.
   d. Determine the visual representation of the word as it relates to the time frame of that historical period.
   e. Determine the function of the word as it relates to the historical period.
2. Examine the change:
   a. Determine what caused the item and the name of the vocabulary word to change over the course of history.
   b. Identify the modern word that matches the antiquated word.

FIGURE 41–1 A sample Brochure for *Buckboard*.

Buckboard

From *Pink and Say* by Patricia Polacco:
We were loaded in a buckboard and taken through town.

My words:
Pink and Say were put in a large wooden wagon without a cover and taken through town.

Dictionary Definition:
Buckboard: A light, four-wheeled carriage in which a long board or lattice frame is used to transport people or supplies.

Function:
A buckboard was used to haul or transport people and supplies. This type of wagon was smaller than a freight wagon that could carry very heavy items, and larger than a carriage that people used to ride into town or go to church. The buckboard relied on horses to pull it.

The Change:
Buckboards were replaced when the combustible engine was designed. Automobiles and trucks became the modes of transportation people used instead of buckboards. People also use vans, minivans, and utility vehicles.

3. Design the "Time Warp" brochure:
    a. Take the information from the word of the past and place it at the top of the brochure.
    b. Add your visual representation of the word.
    c. Include all information about a word that has the present-day similar meaning or usage at the bottom of your brochure (see Figure 41–1).

CONCLUSION

Because our world changes rapidly, our students are less frequently exposed to items of the past and to the words that represent them. They find it hard to believe that people were able to live in a world that didn't have the technology and machines we have now. I feel that it is important for them to analyze the change and see how far we have advanced as a country and dream about the future. Someday their grandchildren will wonder how they were able to live in a world so different from their own.

REFERENCE

Polacco, P. (1994). *Pink and Say*. New York: Philomel Books.

CREATING STUDENT LEXICOLOGISTS

Malisa Ervin

The origins of words, although inherently interesting to a linguist or lover of language, is not really that interesting to the majority of students who are not fascinated by whether a word is derived from Greek or Latin. However, there are some words that have an interesting story behind them. Students are interested in the origins of slang terms they think originated in their generation but have an older history. I share some of the entries from Charles E. Funk's *Thereby Hangs a Tale* (1985) and from *www.takeourword.com* to pique student interest.

PROCEDURE

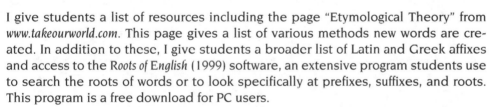

I give students a list of resources including the page "Etymological Theory" from *www.takeourworld.com*. This page gives a list of various methods new words are created. In addition to these, I give students a broader list of Latin and Greek affixes and access to the *Roots of English* (1999) software, an extensive program students use to search the roots of words or to look specifically at prefixes, suffixes, and roots. This program is a free download for PC users.

Next, I show students how they can combine prefixes, roots, and suffixes to create new words such as: *loquaver* combines *loqu* (speak) and *ver* (truth) and–*er* (person who) or *verivocator* for one who speaks truth. I explain how instead of *loquaverer*, which sounds awkward, I could eliminate the last–*er* and change pronunciation but still maintain the meaning. In fact, such changes are often made. I explain that in the same manner, they can dissect a word that is new to them by examining the affixes and roots to approximate its meaning.

After exploring combining roots and affixes to create new words, students examine other means by which words are introduced into our vocabulary. Students may pick a company that seems to outshine others so that the company's name will become synonymous with the product like *Kleenex* has. For example, *google* as a verb has now been added to the dictionary. Tony Hawk seems to be the most popular and greatest advocate for his sport so he could be used.

I put students in pairs and give them 10 vocabulary words (*quadruped, subcutaneous, interpersonal, contraindication, circumnavigate, benefactor, bibliophile, hyperbole, cacophony,* and *metacognition*) that are derived from Greek, Latin, and Anglo-Saxon roots and affixes. Using their resources—dictionaries are not allowed—they are to approximate the meaning of the word. If students are familiar with the definition of the word, they will break the word into its morphemes and approximate the meaning of the morphemes. We then discuss the words as a class with a focus on the changes the words underwent in combining the morphemes. For example, *eccentric* actually

FIGURE 42–1   New Words
Created by Students

New Word	Definition	Method
boodapaching	drumroll and symbol smack	imitation of sound
bocket	back pocket	portmanteau
snospo	snow sports	portmanteau
the clark	a ponytail with no surrounding hair (a style one of our teachers sports)	names
portheo	carry god, uphold god	root + suffix
dictopoly	one who tells many	root + suffix
hyperpel	to drive over	root + suffix
benebilio	a good book	root + suffix

derives from the Greek *ektos* and from Latin *centrum*. E*ktos* is shortened to *ect* (outside of), *centrum* is changed to *centric* (center), and the *t* is removed, creating *eccentric*—outside of center—which we now use to mean odd or unusual. E*ctcentric* is awkward and does not work but *eccentric* is fine. See Figure 42–1 for student-created words and the method they used to make the words.

Finally, I have students create five new words, using at least three different methods outlined in "Etymological Theory," (Melanie & Mike: 2006). They must write down the definition of the words and the technique they used. The students share the new words in a sentence and the class tries to guess the meaning of the newly coined terms. I may also offer extra credit to the one who creates the most words.

CONCLUSION

When we discuss words, students love to introduce terms that are new to me, but are used by teenagers often. During a lesson on denotation versus connotation, students introduced me to the term *dimepiece*, which meant a person who scores a 10 on an attractiveness scale. Although these new words give students an appreciation of the flexibility and versatility of our language, they still do not understand the full richness of a language that has such diverse origins. Playing with the Greek and Latin roots to create new words as well as other methods of creating words opens them up to the history of our language as well as possible future entries.

REFERENCES

Cotter, E. (1999). *Roots of English: An etymological dictionary* Classics Technology Center. Seton Hall University. Retrieved September 22, 2006, from http://ablemedia.com/ctcweb/showcase/roots.html#roots.

Funk, C. (1985). *Thereby hangs a tale*. New York: Harper & Row.

Melanie and Mike. (2006). Etymological theory. *Take our word for it*. Retrieved August 27, 2006, from http://www.takeourword.com/theory.html.

Playing with Words

Teachers understand that if students are to comprehend words at the deepest level, they need multiple contacts with the word. Word games give students new contexts for interaction with words. When students manipulate words in word play they move towards what Baker, Simmons, and Kame'enui (1995) call the *generative* level of understanding. It is at this third and final level when students are able to understand the nuances and connotations of a word; they are able to facilely use the word in their own speech and writing.

In this era of standards-based learning, the word *play* sometimes connotes a frivolousness we are unable to justify, but researchers are clear: Playing with words is a necessary characteristic of vocabulary development. Marzano (2004) describes the seventh characteristic of effective vocabulary instruction: "Students should play with words" (p. 87). He continues by stating, "one powerful technique that schools typically underuse is games" (p. 87). In this review of the recent research concerning vocabulary games, he explains how games "provide challenges" to students, "arouse curiosity," and "help stimulate students' thinking."

This final section contains activities that challenge students through vocabulary play. Janice Peltzer and Lesa Irick have shared activities that encourage students to think beyond definition and use words in creative formats.

Gail Tompkins ("Curing Homophone Madness" and "Word Clusters: Exploring the Multiple Meanings of Words") and Diane Highbaugh present activities that arouse students' curiosity. It is this play with multiple meanings, roots and affixes, and homophones that give students the experience of manipulating words for deeper understanding.

Cathy Blanchfield, Gayle Taylor, and Esther Koers-Hansen describe activities that encourage students to think about words and their meanings. Students think through how words are used and begin to apply this new vocabulary in their own speech and writing.

REFERENCES

Baker, S., Simmons D., & Kame'enui, E. (1995). *Vocabulary acquisition: Synthesis of research*. Eugene, OR: National Center to Improve the Tools of Educators.

Marzano, R. J. (2004). *Building background knowledge for academic achievement: Research on what works in schools*. Alexandria, VA: Association for Supervision and Curriculum Development.

LOGOCREATOLOGY

43

Diane Highbaugh

I believe that if we understand how to break words down into their elemental parts and if we learn the meanings of the various parts, we have learned the secret code of language. By studying Greek word roots, some of the mysteries of the English language are deciphered.

Why not recombine word parts, adding some common words and a smattering of affixes, and fashion our own words? We would then be word creators, or "logocreatologists"!

I spend a concentrated time teaching students about the code of Greek word roots so they become familiar with how many of our words are constructed. I extend this study by encouraging students to invent their own words. The students are empowered to use words creatively while also gaining mastery over the building blocks of the English language.

PROCEDURE

We follow these steps in learning about the Greek language and its influence on many of our English words:

1. Students quickwrite about their own likes, dislikes, fears, dreams, questions, and wonders. The quickwrites could be done over a number of days for younger students, using one topic at a time.
2. The teacher passes out the root words list to each student. *The Reading Teacher's Book of Lists* (Fry, Kress, & Fountoukidis, 2006) is a wonderful resource for lists of roots.
3. Students review their quickwrites and circle 5 to 10 ideas for which they want to create words.
4. Students begin combining root words with common words and affixes.
5. Students check the dictionary to see if their invented words already exist.
6. Students choose two words they've created and put each in the form of a dictionary entry.
7. Students write the word in a sentence, showing how it is used in context.
8. On index cards, students write the dictionary entry of the word and a sentence using the word on one side and the word on the other (see Figure 43–1).
9. The class shares these new words with each other. Students present their word orally to the class, and classmates try to decode the meaning.

FIGURE 43–1 Two
"Logocreatology"
Word Cards

pizzavore (pet'se-vor') n. Eating pizza frequently or in large quantities.
    -**pizzivorous**, adj.

My brother is a **pizzavore**; he likes plain cheese and Hawaiian style the best.

videophile (vid'e-o-fil') n. A lover of videotaped movies watched on a small screen.

My friend Melinda could watch movies day and night at home on her VCR. She is a **videophile**.

CONCLUSION

I collect the index cards in a file box for use as a reference by the class. New words are constantly added to our language and dictionary. For those students who are intrigued as to how words are added to the dictionary, I refer them to the Merriam-Webster website: *www.m-w.com*.

REFERENCE

Fry, E., Kress, J., & Fountoukidis, D. (2006). *The reading teacher's book of lists*. (5th ed.). West Nyack, NY: Prentice Hall.

CURING HOMOPHONE MADNESS

44

Gail Tompkins

Homophones drive my students crazy! These pairs or trios of words sound alike but are spelled differently: Students confuse *hair* and *hare*; others mix up *wood* and *would*, *it's* and *its*, or *right* and *write*; and almost everyone confuses *there*, *their*, and *they're*. A list of homophones is presented in Figure 44–1. Because my students often focus on sound rather than on meaning, they write the more familiar spelling of the word and rarely ask themselves whether they have used the correct spelling.

Most homophones are linguistic accidents—they were never intended to be pronounced the same; *stationary* and *stationery*, however, share an interesting history. S*tationery*, meaning paper and books, developed from the word *stationary*. In medieval England, merchants traveled from town to town selling their wares. The merchant who sold paper goods was the first to set up shop in a town. His shop was "stationary" because it did not move, and he came to be called the "stationer." The spelling difference between the two words signifies the semantic difference.

Many books of homophones are available today, including Fred Gwynne's *The King Who Rained* (2006), *A Chocolate Moose for Dinner* (1998), and *A Little Pigeon Toad* (1988); *What in the World Is a Homophone?* (Presson, 2005); *How much can a Bare Bear Bear?* (Cleary, 2005); and *Eight Ate: A Feast of Homonym Riddles* (Terban, 2007).

Although teachers in the primary grades usually introduce the concept of homophones and teach the easier pairs, including *see–sea*, *I–eye*, *right–write*, and *dear–deer*. Older students, and especially English learners, continue to confuse the more sophisticated pairs, including *morning–mourning*, *flair–flare*, and *complement–compliment*.

Intensive study is often necessary because homophones are confusing. The words sound alike and the spellings are often very similar—sometimes only one letter varies or one letter is added: *wave–waive* and *naval–navel*.

As a part of a unit on homophones, I have my students make a class collaboration book about homophones that is placed in the classroom library. I've found that having a reference book helps my students become more careful when they are writing homophones. A page from a seventh-grade class book is shown in Figure 44–2. On each page in the book, students wrote the homophone pairs or trios, drew pictures to illustrate each word, and used each word in a sentence.

PROCEDURE

The steps in creating a class collaboration book on homophones include the following:

1. Brainstorm a list of homophone pairs and trios with the students and write them on a chart to post in the classroom.

153

air–heir	coarse–course	hoarse–horse	pause–paws	shoot–chute
allowed–aloud	colonel–kernel	hoes–hose	peace–piece	side–sighed
ball–bawl	complement–	hole–whole	peak–peek–pique	sighs–size
band–banned	compliment	jam–jamb	peal–peel	slay–sleigh
bare–bear	council–counsel	knead–need	pedal–peddle	soar–sore
base–bass	creak–creek	knight–night	peer–pier	soared–sword
based–baste	days–daze	knot–not	phase–faze	sole–soul
beat–beet	dense–dents	lacks–lax	plain–plane	stairs–stares
bell–belle	dew–do–due	lead–led	plait–plate	stake–steak
berry–bury	die–dye	leak–leek	pleas–please	stationary–stationery
berth–birth	doe–dough	leased–least	pole–poll	steal–steel
billed–build	dual–duel	lie–lye	pore–pour	straight–strait
blew–blue	ewe–you	links–linx	praise–prays–preys	suite–sweet
boar–bore	fair–fare	load–lode	presence–presents	tail–tale
board–bored	feat–feet	loan–lone	pride–pried	taught–taut
boarder–border	fined–find	loot–lute	prince–prints	tear–tier
born–borne	flea–flee	mail–male	principal–principle	tense–tents
bough–bow	flew–flu	main–mane	profit–prophet	their–there–they're
brake–break	floe–flow	maize–maze	quarts–quartz	threw–through
bread–bred	flour–flower	manner–manor	rain–rein–reign	throne–thrown
brews–bruise	foaled–fold	marshal–martial	raise–rays–raze	tide–tied
bridal–bridle	for–fore–four	meat–meet–mete	rap–wrap	toad–toed–towed
brows–browse	forth–fourth	medal–meddle–metal	real–reel	toe–tow
cache–cash	foul–fowl	might–mite	red–read	tracked–tract
callous–callus	gait–gate	mind–mined	rest–wrest	troop–troupe
capital–capitol	genes–jeans	miner–minor	right–rite–write	undo–undue
carat–carrot	gofer–gopher	missed–mist	ring–wring	vain–vane–vein
cast–caste	gorilla–guerrilla	moan–mown	road–rode–rowed	wade–weighed
cede–seed	grate–great	moose–mousse	role–roll	waist–waste
ceiling–sealing	grill–grille	morning–mourning	roomer–rumor	wait–weight
cell–sell	groan–grown	muscle–mussel	root–route	waive–wave
cellar–seller	guessed–guest	naval–navel	rose–rows	wares–wears
cent–scent–sent	hail–hale	none–nun	rote–wrote	warn–worn
chews–choose	hair–hare	oar–or–ore	rung–wrung	way–weigh
chic–sheik	hall–haul	paced–paste	sac–sack	weak–week
chili–chilly	halve–have	packed–pact	scene–seen	wood–would
choral–coral	hangar–hanger	pail–pale	sealing–ceiling	yoke–yolk
chord–cord–cored	hay–hey	pain–pane	seam–seem	
chute–shoot	heal–heel	pair–pare–pear	serf–surf	
cite–sight–site	heard–herd	palette–pallet	sew–so–sow	
clause–claws	heroin–heroine	passed–past	shear–sheer	
close–clothes	hoard–horde	patience–patients	shone–shown	

FIGURE 44–1   A List of Homophones

2. Have students each select a homophone pair or trio to illustrate and write their names next to the words.
3. Have students review the meanings of the homophone words in a dictionary in preparation for making the illustrations.
4. Have students design their homophone book pages and write the words, draw illustrations for each word, and use each word in a sentence.
5. Hold a whole-class revising/editing session to review each student's page and assist the students in making corrections as needed.
6. Collect the pages and arrange them in alphabetical order.

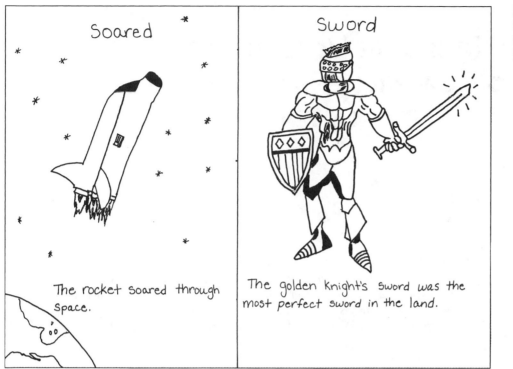

Soared

The rocket soared through space.

Sword

The golden knight's sword was the most perfect sword in the land.

FIGURE 44–2 A Page from a Seventh-Grade Class Book on Homophones

7. Have a student make a cover for the book and laminate it so that it will last longer.
8. Bind the book using brads, ribbon, or clips.

APPLICATIONS

I like to make the homophone books as part of a unit on homophones, and several times during the unit, I give students a quiz about homophone usage. We correct these quizzes together, and students identify the homophones that confuse them. I then encourage students to make individual books of the homophones that continue to confuse them, and they refer to these books throughout the school year.

CONCLUSION

Homophones are difficult for students because the pairs and trios of words are pronounced the same even though they are spelled differently. If students pay more attention to the sounds of words than to the meanings of words when they are writing, they are likely to make homophone errors. The best way I've found to cure the homophone madness is to directly teach students about homophones and have them study the homophones that are confusing. Making class books illustrating the pairs and trios of "sound alike" words is an important step in my instructional practice.

REFERENCES

Cleary, B. P. (2005). *How much can a bare bear bear?* Minneapolis, MN: Millbrook Press.
Gwynne, F. (1988). *A little pigeon toad.* New York: Simon & Schuster.
Gwynne, F. (1998). *A chocolate moose for dinner.* New York: Windmill Books.
Gwynne, F. (2006). *The king who rained.* New York: Windmill Book.
Presson, L. (2005). *What in the world is a homophone?* New York: Barron's.
Terban, M. (2007). *Eight ate: A feast of homonym riddles.* New York: Clarion Books.

45

BUILDING VOCABULARY AND COMPREHENSION THROUGH DRAMATIZATION

Janice Peltzer

Back-to-School Night is held the second week of school in our district. Parents often ask, "What kind of vocabulary program do your students have? Will they have weekly vocabulary tests?" When I explain to them that I like to teach vocabulary in context using drama for understanding, they don't always comprehend how this works. The easiest way for them to understand is for me to show them.

Several years ago, I went to a reading conference where I received a copy of an article entitled "Man of Letters," from *People* (1998). It is the story of a man who learned to read late in life. He entered an adult literacy class at the age of 98 and by the time he turned 100, he could read at the third-grade level. Because it is short and to the point, I use it as an example of vocabulary and comprehension building.

PROCEDURE

The first thing I do is pass out the article face down. I tell the students that they cannot turn it over until I ring the bell. When the bell is rung, they are to look at the picture and words to see if they can figure out what the article might be about. I quickly ring the bell again and they must turn the paper back over. This is very brief and quick; less than 5 seconds. Then the students make a prediction about the article. What is it about? Who is it about? When did it happen, and so forth? The students readily get involved in this activity. We continue in this manner, looking next at the bold printed words and the smaller printed words, and then we prepare to read the article.

Before reading the article, I give students each a sticky note on which they are to write the words they do not recognize or understand. In this article, the students came up with a list of eight words that they were not familiar with: *siblings, grueling, decades, literacy, enroll, ties, illiteracy,* and *spike.* I write the words on the chalkboard as the students share words from their lists with the class. Students notice that they know the word *ties,* so why was it on the list? As the class looked at the word in context, they saw that it did not make sense with their prior knowledge of the word. Therefore, they had to find out the correct definition of the word so that it would make sense in this context.

After the students have their lists compiled, they work together in groups of two or three students to consult the dictionary to find the correct definitions of all eight words and write them down. As they are working on the words, they talk about the correct definition based on how it is used in the sentence. They ask themselves, "Does this meaning make sense in the sentence? Do I understand the word?

156

Dear Mr. Dawson,

In our sixth-grade class at school, we read an article about you that was published in *People* magazine. I really felt bad when I found out that you never got to learn to read. I learned to read in kindergarten. You can be proud of yourself that you are no longer illiterate.

Just like you, I come from a family of siblings; three brothers and a sister. Even though we get mad at one another, we love each other a lot. This summer we are all going to enroll at the YMCA and take swimming lessons. I don't know how to swim very well.

I have a question about the grueling work you did on the railroad. How heavy were those railroad ties? I didn't understand what a railroad tie was until we read your letter and looked up the word in the dictionary. The only tie I am familiar with is the one my dad wears to church on Sunday.

I also didn't know what the word "spike" meant, but it is like a big nail that the railroad ties were fastened with. The dictionary has twenty meanings for the word "spike," but some friends and I figured out which definition worked best for the word.

You are a great example to me! After reading your article, I went home and told my family about it. I decided that if you can learn to read at 98, I can learn to be a better swimmer. Thank you for your article.

Sincerely,

Carey

FIGURE 45–1   Sample Student Letter

Is there another word I know that has the same meaning? How else could the word be used?"

When the students are finished, I explain that they are going to become actors. Their job is to work in groups of three to four to act out a vocabulary word for the class. Students cannot talk, but they can use props to help them in their dramatization. I give them time and supplies to work out their ideas. The students come up with some very clever ways of presenting their words to the class.

This is an activity where all students participate enthusiastically, even if they are just playing the part of a chair. It is the job of the audience to figure out the word that is being portrayed, to be respectful of the other students, and to be involved in the learning process. I have found this to be a very successful strategy.

As a concluding activity with the new vocabulary words, students each write a letter to Mr. Dawson, the man in the article. In their letters, they are to include at least five of the new vocabulary words and use them correctly in their sentences. Figure 45–1 is a letter one of my sixth graders wrote to Mr. Dawson.

As students write their letters, the words have greater meaning to them, increasing their comprehension while adding to their vocabulary.

CONCLUSION

I have found that this same process also works well using several pages or chapters in a novel, in reading short stories, studying history or science chapters, or reading articles in the newspaper.

REFERENCE

"Man of letters." (1998, April 6). *People*, 51(40), 112.

VOCABULARY POETRY: A MEANS OF ASSESSMENT

Lesa Irick

Vocabulary poetry is a creative alternative to multiple-choice, fill-in-the-blank, or write-the-definition-of tests. It is a means of assessment that involves creating poetry using vocabulary words and prepositions. Using this combination of prepositions and selected vocabulary words from a single piece of literature, chapter, or unit allows students to demonstrate their knowledge of the vocabulary words by using them contextually in a poem.

This lesson is very useful in determining whether or not the students comprehend their vocabulary words. Allowing them the freedom to be creative enables them to visualize with the poet. You will be amazed at the re-creations of the text the students will generate.

PROCEDURE

After we have read a text using a variety of comprehension and vocabulary study exercises, I follow these steps:

1. Students must have their vocabulary words and definitions, text containing the vocabulary words, student worksheet (see Figure 46–1), and preposition list (see Figure 46–2).

FIGURE 46–1 Student Directions

Vocabulary Poetry Test

Name_____

Title of literature_____

Using your vocabulary words, definitions, and prepositions from your list, you are going to create a poem that will demonstrate your knowledge of the vocabulary words.

Directions: Choose one vocabulary word; for example, a*byss*—a deep or bottomless pit. Next, choose a preposition that corresponds to that vocabulary word; for example, *into.* Connect the two to come up with an interesting prepositional phrase; for example, *into the dark, lifeless abyss.* Continue until you have used all of your vocabulary words. You may add key words from the literature to help create meaning, but they also must be paired with a preposition. You may not quote directly from the text. When your phrases are complete, you can rearrange them to create an interesting poem. Please underline each vocabulary word.

FIGURE **46–2** List of Prepositions

Prepositions

about	below	in back of	of
above	beneath	in front of	off
according to	beside	in regard to	past
across	between	in spite of	prior to
after	by	inside	since
against	down	instead of	through
along with	due to	into	to
among	during	like	under
around	except	near	until
as	except for	next to	up
at	for	on	with
because of	from	on account of	within
before	in	outside	without

2. Briefly review prepositions. A preposition is a word or group of words that shows the relationship between a noun or pronoun and some other word in the sentence.
3. Explain to students that they are going to demonstrate their knowledge of the vocabulary words by creating a poem that will serve as a retelling of the literature.
4. Direct students to pair up one vocabulary word with one preposition, creating a prepositional phrase. No direct quotes from literature are allowed; ask students to use their newly created prepositional phrases in the poem.
5. Once the phrases are completed, have students manipulate them to create a retelling of the literature.
6. Have students create a final draft free of errors.

One of my students chose *sagacity, dissimulate, dismember, gesticulations,* and *corpse* as important vocabulary words from "The Tell-Tale Heart," by Edgar Allan Poe (1963), and created this poem using the words:

On Account of the Evil Eye
Due to foresight and <u>dissimulation</u>,
With a great <u>sagacity</u>,
Because of the <u>corpse's</u> eye,
A bed over the <u>dismembered</u> body.
Beneath the floorboards,
On account of violent <u>gesticulations</u>,
To seal my fate.

CONCLUSION

Creating a poem by manipulating text presents a totally new twist to the literature and allows students to experience what they are reading through the author's eyes as well as their own. They begin to use some of the vocabulary to express meaning, and through their poetry, I can assess how well they are understanding the literature.

REFERENCE

Hoban, R. (1963). *Tales and poems of Edgar Allan Poe.* New York: Macmillan.

47

WORD CLUSTERS: EXPLORING THE MULTIPLE MEANINGS OF WORDS

Gail Tompkins

It's a fact that most English words have more than one meaning. The word *adverse*, for example, has several related meanings: "to oppose," "contrary to," and "in an opposite direction." These meanings are clearly related, coming from the same Latin root. The related meanings of another word—*sanguine*—aren't so clear, unless you know about medieval physiology. *Sanguine* can be traced back to the Latin word *saguis* meaning "blood." Its meanings include "ruddy," cheerful," "optimistic," and "passionate." Medieval physicians believed that blood was one of the four bodily fluids and that personalities were determined by the relative proportions of these fluids in people's bodies. If blood was predominant, people were red-faced, cheerful, hopeful, and likely to fall in love.

Common, everyday words have even more meanings. Consider these 12 meanings of the word *dull*:

- "stupid," as in a dull boy
- "insensitive," as in a dull comment
- "listless or dispirited," as in feeling dull
- "sluggish," as in business was dull
- "blunt," as in a dull knife
- "lackluster," as in a dull shine
- "not clear," as in a dull thud
- "not keenly felt," as in a dull ache
- "cloudy or overcast," as in a dull day
- "boring," as in a dull story
- "tedious," as in a dull task
- "slightly grayish," as in a dull red

These meanings all come from the same Old English word, *dol*, which has broadened considerably in meaning over the past 1,500 years.

Multiple meanings occur for several reasons. English speakers often create noun and verb forms of a word. For example, *face* has several noun and verb forms: *the face of the city* (n), *she's afraid of losing face* (n), *the building faces west* (v), *soldiers face danger* (v). These meanings are intentionally related; they all come from the same Latin word. Other words with multiple meanings were created accidentally. These words began as different words, but after hundreds of years they are spelled the same way. Often these words entered English from different languages; for example, *file*, meaning "a device for keeping papers and records" (n) or "to arrange in order" (v) entered the English language from the French around 1450. The word *file*, meaning "a long, narrow steel tool for smoothing hard surfaces" (n) or "to rub or smooth with a file" (v), is an older English word that was used before 900 A.D. Other words come from the same language but were separate words and originally spelled differently. Consider the two meanings of *yard*: "a unit of linear measurement" and "the land that surrounds a house." Both are English words that were originally spelled differently. The word meaning "a unit of measurement" was spelled *gerd* in Old English and meant a "straight twig," and the word meaning "the land surrounding a house" came from a different Old English word spelled *geard*, meaning "enclosure." It's not surprising that over time, the words were spelled the same even though their meanings are not related. Figurative uses of words, such as idioms, create additional meanings for words.

If you're interested in learning about the meanings of words and how the words entered English, you need to check an unabridged dictionary; a separate entry is provided for each word with a unique word history. *Random House Webster's Unabridged Dictionary* (2005) lists three entries for *scale*, for example. Each entry comes from a different language. The meanings "an instrument for weighing" (n) and "to weight on scales" (v) come from an Old Norse word meaning "bowl." The meanings "one of the small stiff plates that cover an animal's body" (n) and "to flake or remove the scales from an animal's body" (v) come from an old Germanic word meaning "shell." These other meanings come from a Latin word meaning "ladder": "a series of tones going up or down in pitch" (n); "a series of paces marked off by lines and used for measuring distances or amounts" (n); "the size of a picture, plan, or model of a thing compared to the size of the thing itself" (n); or "to climb by or as if by a ladder" (v). The meanings are presented and then etymological information, enclosed in brackets, is provided at the end of the entry. The etymological information explains how and when the word entered English, and it is useful for understanding some of the seemingly unrelated meanings of words.

Janet Allen (1999) explained that when students learn vocabulary, they move from knowing how to use a word in a single context to a richer, more complete knowledge of the word, including understanding its multiple meanings. Word learning is complex; students gradually develop a more complete knowledge of a word (Beck, McKeown, & Kucan, 2002). They learn about the multiple meanings of sophisticated words like *adverse* and *sanguine* as well as more common, but still confusing, words like *dull, face, file,* and *scale*. English learners, in particular, are often confused by unfamiliar meanings of everyday words. Fay and Whaley (2004) list words with multiple meanings as one of the challenges for English learners and suggest that teachers teach students about the unfamiliar meanings of words.

PROCEDURE

Word clusters are a good way to focus students' attention on the multiple meanings of a word. Graphic representations show relationships more clearly than dictionary entries can. The word is written at the top or in the center of a box or circle, and then the meanings are written next to rays drawn out from the box or circle. Students can use a combination of drawings and words to explain the meanings. A sixth grader's cluster for *current*, explaining three meanings for the word, is presented in Figure 47–1.

The steps in making a word cluster to highlight the multiple meanings of a word include:

1. Choose a word to study and write it at the top or in the center of a sheet of paper or on a poster. Draw a box or a circle around the word.
2. Review the meanings of the word in a dictionary and decide which meanings to represent on the word cluster.
3. Draw out rays from the word box or circle and write the definition and/or draw a picture to illustrate the meaning. Sometimes students also identify

FIGURE 47–1 Student's
Word Cluster for *Current*

the part of speech or explain the etymology (or word history) of each
meaning.
4. Add a sentence to illustrate each meaning.
5. Share completed word clusters with classmates and display them in the
classroom.

EXTENSION

Many words have 5, 10, or even 20 or more meanings. Think about the word *bad* and
its meanings. How many meanings can you think of? *Random House Webster's
Unabridged Dictionary* (2005) lists 47 meanings for *bad*, including:

- "not good," as in bad weather
- "not favorable," as in a bad impression
- "not fresh," as in bad fish
- "morally evil," as in a bad person
- "not enough," as in bad lighting
- "unpleasant," as in bad news
- "harmful," as in bad for your health
- "severe," as in a bad cold
- "not correct," as in bad spelling
- "sick," as in a cold makes you feel bad
- "sorry," as in feeling bad about a mistake

FIGURE 47–2 A List of Common Words with More Than Five Meanings

act	air	around	away	boat	cut
affect	all right	black	blow	catch	fair
bar	base	case	cast	color	good
capital	carry	clear	close	crown	high
charge	check	crack	cross	drive	just
court	cover	draw	dress	fail	leave
dead	deep	fight	face	fly	let
dull	even	head	fire	heel	lie
effect	fast	hot	have	lay	measure
green	hand	knock	house	mark	nose
hold	horn	make	know	part	pass
keep	key	natural	man	pipe	pitch
line	low	number	new	play	point
mind	mine	over	paper	put	quiet
note	now	picture	piece	rear	rest
open	out	plant	plate	ring	rise
pay	pick	power	print	scale	score
place	plain	principal	reach	shift	section
positive	post	range	right	side	shine
rain	raise	ride	run	slip	sight
return	rich	rule	sharp	spread	small
roll	round	set	show	stay	spring
send	serve	shot	sit	strike	step
shoot	short	sink	spin	swing	stroke
sign	sing	sound	start	think	switch
snap	stamp	star	stop	twist	through
square	stiff	stock	sweet	way	touch
stick	stuff	sweep	thing	bank	under
strong	take	thick	time	break	wear
tack	tie	tight	turn	change	weather
throw	train	trip	watch	counsel	weigh
tough	use	warm	bad	count	wreck

Other common words with more than five meanings, such as *around, count, measure,* and *section,* are shown in Figure 47–2. Middle school students often know two or three meanings, but when they make a word cluster, their word knowledge deepens. A seventh-grade word cluster for *hot* is shown in Figure 47–3. The students made this cluster on a large poster and drew pictures to illustrate 10 meanings of the word.

CONCLUSION

Learning the multiple meanings of both common, everyday words and more sophisticated words is an important part of students' vocabulary development in grades 6–12. Teachers draw students' attention to the multiple meanings of words in different ways, by having them make word clusters. As students make word clusters, they deepen their knowledge of words and begin to appreciate that English is an evolving language where words continue to acquire new meanings as people use them in new ways.

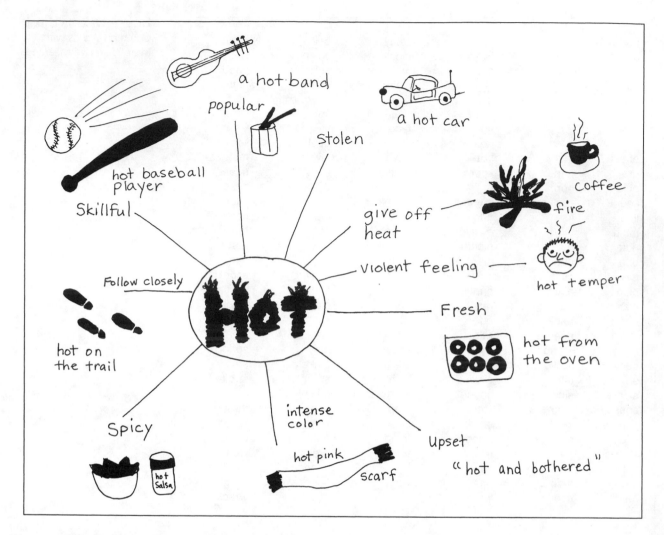

FIGURE 47–3 Seventh Grader's Cluster of 10 Meanings of *Hot*

REFERENCES

Allen, J. (1999). *Words, words words: Teaching vocabulary in grades 4–12*. York, ME: Stenhouse.

Beck, I. I., McKeown, M. G., & Kucan, L. (2002). *Bringing words to life: Robust vocabulary instruction*. New York: Guilford Press.

Fay, K., & Whaley, S. (2004). *Becoming one community: Reading and writing with English language learners*. Portland, ME: Stenhouse.

Random House Webster's unabridged dictionary. (2nd ed.). (2005). New York: Random House.

Vocabulary Crosswords

Cathy Blanchfield

Adolescents love games and puzzles. They especially love creating puzzles, and then working out each other's. Often, throughout the year, my students play games with words. Usually these games are reinforcing activities, played after extensive teaching of the vocabulary to be used in the game. Vocabulary crosswords are not necessarily used after teaching. They can be created by students in the initial stages of learning new words.

PROCEDURE

My students live in a low-socioeconomic area and often have never seen a crossword puzzle. For this reason, I complete the first puzzle of the year on the overhead with the whole class. The following day, I have copies of the puzzle made so all can complete the puzzle at their desks. In this way, we learn to create the puzzles as well as learn strategies for completing them.

After about a week, I give the students a new set of words and ask them to work in groups to create a puzzle. They look up the words in a dictionary and discuss the meanings. They write the clues for the puzzle from these negotiated definitions. All groups have the same words, but, of course, their puzzles will look different. Then we exchange puzzles and the new groups now attempt to complete the puzzles. If a group has difficulty completing the puzzle, they write a note to the original group. In this way, misunderstandings are corrected, multiple meanings are discovered, and the meanings of this new vocabulary are reinforced.

Later in the year, students make puzzles individually. All students are given the same words and are allowed to work as a group to find the meanings of the words. Then, they make individual puzzles following the steps shown in the student handout. The student handout for a section of *The Fighting Ground*, by Avi, shown in Figure 48–1, reviews these steps:

1. Connect the words (individually)
2. Find the meaning of the words (in groups)
3. Make the boxes for the puzzle
4. Write in the numbers
5. Write the meanings as clues

We exchange puzzles, again to find any misconceptions, discuss new definitions, and reinforce learning. Figure 48–2 shows a student's puzzle for *The Fighting Ground*.

FIGURE 48–1 Crossword
Puzzle Directions

THE FIGHTING GROUND
Vocabulary—pp. 58–67

Make a puzzle with the following words:

     intently
     cautious
     curious
     reply
     humiliation
     vanish
     originally
     menacingly

Follow these steps:

    1. Connect all of the words so that no words touch each other except when they share a letter:

```
      curious
      a
      u
      t
      i
      o
      u
vanish
```

    This is your answer sheet.

    2. Find the meaning of each word. Be sure to write definitions in your own words.

    3. Count the letters in each word and draw boxes on another piece of paper. Make sure the boxes connect at the proper places so someone else can fill in the right words.

    4. Write a number in the first box of each word.

    5. Write the meanings for the words as clues.

OTHER POSSIBILITIES

As a postreading activity, the students can choose 8 or 10 words from a list of words that were studied during the unit. Then when the students trade vocabulary, each student reviews both the words that he or she chose and those in the second puzzle. This adds the variety needed in order to test the students' comprehension after the unit.

    This activity is excellent for content-area teachers. The activity described would fit well into science or history classes. Another variety of puzzle uses pictures. In math, the clues can be drawings instead of word definitions; a clue for *rectangle*, then, would be: ▭. In art, the clues could be colors; the clue for *magenta* would be a spot of the color magenta.

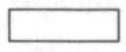

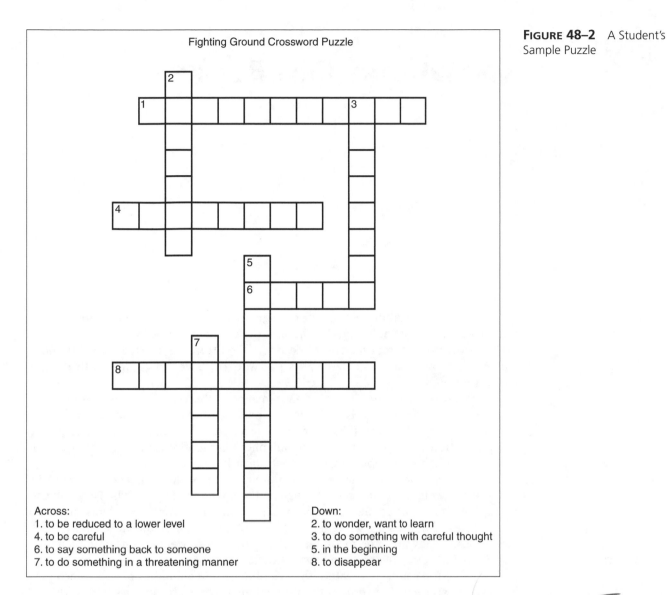

Fighting Ground Crossword Puzzle

FIGURE 48–2 A Student's Sample Puzzle

Across:
1. to be reduced to a lower level
4. to be careful
6. to say something back to someone
7. to do something in a threatening manner

Down:
2. to wonder, want to learn
3. to do something with careful thought
5. in the beginning
8. to disappear

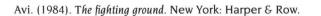

CONCLUSION

Crosswords are a creative way to introduce as well as reinforce and test vocabulary. Students respond positively to this activity, and often when we are finished, they walk in the next day asking if they can do another one.

REFERENCE

Avi. (1984). *The fighting ground.* New York: Harper & Row.

VOCABULARY CRIB BOOKS

Gayle Taylor

Although vocabulary is better taught in context with what students are reading, many schools require assigned vocabulary books by grade level. These words can sometimes be worked into the literature used in class, but more often they must be taught 20 words per week in order to comply with district requirements.

Because words are used to create images in the reader's mind, creating the images to go with the words can help students to remember the definitions. In his book *How the Brain Learns* (2001), David Sousa notes that "using imagery regularly in instruction. . . is a powerful aid to hemisphere integration and retention" (p. 103). I implement this concept in two ways—flashcards and crib books.

For the flashcards, I assign each student one of the 20 district-required words. I have students create images that suggest the meaning of the words. They can use drawings, magazine collages, computer clip art, or photographs. Students then add a sentence that uses the word in the context of the image on the card. On the back of the card, they print the meaning of the word. The students print them on a half-sheet of index paper, and then I laminate them.

Once the cards are created, they can be used in a number of ways. Each day, I have the students form groups of three or four. I give each group a set of cards and allow them about 6 minutes to discuss the pictures and the meanings. The groups exchange cards until all cards have been passed. The cards can be used daily in pairs or groups as flashcards: One student shows the image side of the card, and the partner says the meaning of the word. They take turns "flashing" images, saying meanings, and checking each other's answers. The cards can also be used to play vocabulary baseball or team challenges.

In addition, once the students have created their cards, they can scan their images and save them to a community diskette. Students can print images to create a crib book that can be used during test day. On crib books, only the image and sentence sides can be used. Figure 49–1 shows both sides of a student page.

Crib books are a way to provide students with a study book for vocabulary tests. Students glue the image and sentence sides for each word onto a page of the book. As students turn each page of their book, they see a picture and a sentence clue for each of their vocabulary words; this is a way to review the words. If they find that they have forgotten any of the meanings, they can look back to their flashcards.

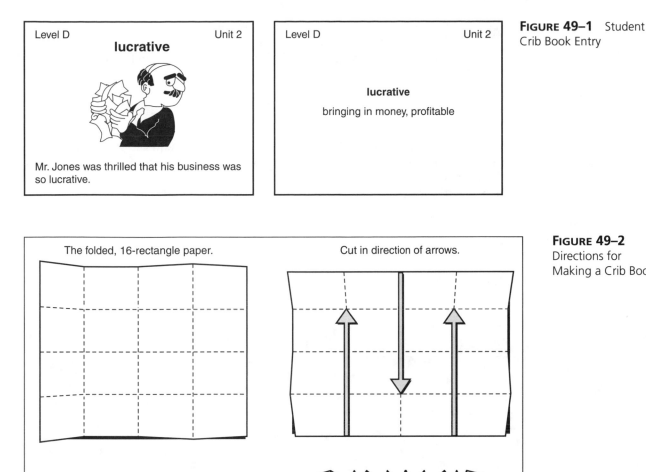

FIGURE 49–1 Student Crib Book Entry

FIGURE 49–2 Directions for Making a Crib Book

PROCEDURE

Follow these directions to create a crib book:

1. Fold a piece of paper (8 ½ × 11 inches or larger) lengthwise by making two "hotdog" folds.
2. Open and fold crosswise by making two "hamburger" folds to create 16 rectangles, as shown in Figure 49–2.
3. Cut between the columns, as shown in Figure 49–2. Between the first and second columns, cut from the bottom, stopping at the bottom of the top row. Between the second and third columns, cut down, stopping at the top of the bottom row. Then, between the third and fourth columns, cut up from the bottom to match the first cut.
4. Pinch together each uncut rectangle pair, folding as shown, to create one long strip with each rectangle pair standing up (see Figure 49–2).

5. Glue these standing rectangles together.
6. Fold from the left, accordian style, to make the booklet.
7. Paste a picture on each page of the book, as shown in Figure 49–2.

CONCLUSION

If I allow students to use crib books for a test, I collect them during the beginning of the period and check for unauthorized words, concepts, or answers, then pass them back just prior to the test. I encourage students to create and use the books because it gives them more time to connect the image to the meaning of the word.

REFERENCE

Sousa, D. (2001). *How the brain learns*. Reston, VA: NAASP.

VOCABULARY TABOO: A PLAYFUL APPROACH TO DENOTATION, CONNOTATION, AND WORD RELATIONSHIPS

Esther Koers-Hansen

Taboo is a word game in which one person is the clue-giver, and the other person is the guesser. The object is for the clue-giver to reveal enough about the "play word" without using the play word itself or any part of the play word so that the guesser can figure out the word. They also may not use the five "taboo" words listed below the play word on the taboo card. The taboo words are synonyms related to the play word that cannot be used to describe or define the play word.

According to Marzano and Pickering (2005), students do not internalize vocabulary until they have had multiple exposures to the words, including opportunities to play with words. They explain that "understanding deepens over time if students continually reexamine their understanding of a given term" (p. 28). This game allows students opportunities to reexamine their understanding of vocabulary. Many times students have a denotative (literal) definition of vocabulary, but they do not understand the connotative (emotional response) meanings evoked by the word. Taboo helps them discover these connotations.

After multiple exposures to a word—students describing it in their own words, visually representing it, using it in their writing or speech, and discussing the connotations of the word—students create a Taboo card for the word.

I usually do this activity when we have a class vocabulary list of at least 10 words. The words are from texts they have read, as well as literary and other content-area terminology they need to know. In order for students to create the list of five "taboo" words, they need to thoroughly understand the denotative and connotative meanings of the words. After they create their cards, we have three "decks" of cards (sometimes more, sometimes less, depending on the size of the class and the vocabulary list) that I keep in self-closing plastic bags and use throughout the year to energize the students.

PROCEDURE

To prepare the decks of cards, follow these steps:

1. Group students in pairs and give each pair a blank 3 × 5 card.
2. Each pair is given one of the words on our list. With a list of 10 vocabulary words, three or more pairs are given the same word. These words become the play words.
3. Students write the word in blue at the top of the card and underline it in red.
4. Students then refer back to the notes and visuals they have created for the play word and come up with five "taboo" words. They may also use a

FIGURE 50–1 Sample
Taboo Cards

FEIGN	SKEPTICAL
Pretend	Doubt
Two-faced	Believe
False	Proof
Lie	Question
Story	Convince

FIGURE 50–2 Organization
of Students for Playing the
Game

Group 1	Group 2	Group 3
AA	AA	AA
BB	BB	BB
CC	CC	CC
DD	DD	DD
EE	EE	EE

Pair AA in each group begins with clue-giving and guessing, while pair BB in each group watches AA's play to make sure that the rules are followed. Then pair BB plays while pair CC watches.

dictionary and thesaurus. Figure 50–1 shows examples of play words and their related taboo words.

5. They list the taboo words under the red line in black ink.

PLAYING THE GAME

To play the game, I pair students and divide the pairs into groups 1, 2, and 3 to correlate with the number of decks of cards we have. If we have three decks of cards, for example, then the class is divided into three groups, consisting of pairs. Each pair is a team, competing against every other team in the class to guess as many play words correctly in the time given. Because each pair is a team working together to give clues about and guess the play word, another team watches their play to make sure that the clue-giver does not use any part of the play word or the "taboo" words to reveal what the play word means. See Figure 50–2 for a visual of how this works.

Each pair has three minutes to give clues and guess the play word. For the word *skeptical* (Figure 50–1), one student told her partner, "Johnny told a story and Mary said no way. So Mary is . . ." and her partner knew the word immediately. The pair who gets it right within the three minutes without using the word, any variation of the word, or a "taboo" word, gets a point.

After playing Taboo, I ask students to evaluate the cards they used in the game. This allows us to clarify misunderstandings of words and meanings or to further delve into multiple meanings and connotations associated with words. Any card deemed problematic, too easy, or insufficient is replaced by a better one with a list of "taboo" words agreed upon by the class.

CONCLUSION

This activity is a way in which students can play and interact with words in several ways: finding synonyms related to the denotation and connotation of the vocabulary word (for example, there is a negative connotation to the word *feign*, which is illustrated by the "taboo" word *two-faced* on the card in Figure 50–1), thinking about and describing vocabulary words in new ways, listening to descriptions of words and having to synthesize that information to think of the words, evaluating the relationships of the related taboo words to the vocabulary word, and evaluating and judging the effectiveness of the denotations and connotations of all six words on the card.

REFERENCE

Marzano, R. J., & Pickering, D. J. (2005). *Building academic vocabulary*. Alexandria, VA: Association for Supervision and Curriculum Development.

ABOUT THE AUTHORS

Cathy Blanchfield is a secondary teacher in the Fresno Unified School District in Fresno, California. She has taught middle and high school students from predominantly low-socioeconomic neighborhoods and is presently serving her high school as a Literacy Lead Teacher. She received her B.A. from the University of California, Berkeley, and her M.A. in Education, Reading emphasis from California State University, Fresno. Cathy serves the San Joaquin Valley Writing Project as a Teacher Consultant and Co-Director.

Eileen Boland has been a classroom teacher for 18 years. Her experiences have been in teaching language arts and history at the middle and high school level. Curriculum design and assessment are her two areas of interest. She holds an M.A. in Education, Reading/Language Arts emphasis, and she spent time at the University of Georgia in postgraduate work. She is a Teacher Consultant for the San Joaquin Valley Writing Project and teaches at Roosevelt High School in the Fresno Unified School District.

Ann Brandon is a teacher at Reedley High School. She earned a B.A. in English and an M.A. in Education, Reading/Language Arts emphasis from California State University, Fresno. Ann has been a Teacher Consultant for the San Joaquin Valley Writing Project since 2002, a Co-Director for the Reading Institute for Academic Preparation (RIAP) for the past 4 years, and continues to serve in a variety of leadership capacities for her school district. In 2005, Ann earned her National Board Certification.

Cathy Cirimele has taught English for over 25 years at the middle school, high school, and community college levels. After receiving her B.A. in English from California State University, Fresno, she earned an M.A. in Literature from San Francisco State and then an M.A. in Education, Reading emphasis from Fresno Pacific College. Currently she teaches English at Bullard High School in Fresno, California, and serves as Co-Director of the Bullard Humanities Project, an interdisciplinary program that integrates technology into humanities-based courses. She serves as a Teacher Consultant for both the California Reading and Literature Project and the San Joaquin Valley Writing Project.

Martha Dudley was a beloved literature, language arts, and social studies teacher at Abraham Lincoln Middle School in Selma, California. She was a Teacher Consultant for the San Joaquin Valley Writing Project and a participant in the National Writing Project's "Focus on Standards." Martha often represented teachers at state-level meetings. Everyone was saddened when Martha passed away in the fall of 2003.

Malisa Ervin has taught at Bullard High School in the Fresno Unified School District, Fresno, California, for more than 11 years. She is currently teaching junior English and levels I, II and III English language development. She is part of the Humanities program, where she enjoys working with other teachers at Bullard in integrating technology and developing curriculum across the disciplines. In addition, she has participated in the California Professional Development Institute and the FIELD project sponsored by the California International Studies Project. Malisa is a Teacher Consultant for the San Joaquin Valley Writing Project.

Kathleen Godfrey is an associate professor of English at California State University, Fresno, and Co-Director of the San Joaquin Valley Writing Project. Before earning her Ph.D. in American Literature, she taught middle school in the Long Beach Unified School District. She has published a number of articles on women's writing in such journals as *Western American Literature* and *Southwestern American Literature*.

Laurie Goodman is the principal of Rafer Johnson Junior High School in the Kings Canyon Unified School District. She has served as a literacy coach and taught eighth grade in Hanford, California. She has an M.A. in Education, Reading/Language Arts emphasis from California State University, Fresno, and she is currently a doctoral student at the University of California, Davis/California State University, Fresno Joint Doctoral Program. She has been a Teacher Consultant with the San Joaquin Valley Writing Project since 1995.

Tamara Harritt taught for almost 30 years in kindergarten through eighth grade, and she is now retired. Tamara holds an M.A. in Education, Reading/Language Arts emphasis, from the University of San Francisco and is an alumna of California State University, Fresno. She is a Teacher Consultant in the San Joaquin Valley Writing Project.

Diane Highbaugh has taught in the Selma Unified School District in Selma, California, since 1995. She currently teaches language arts and history to middle school students. Diane is a Teacher Consultant in the San Joaquin Valley Writing Project and is an avid reader of children's and young adult literature.

Lesa Irick, a California State University, Fresno, graduate, teaches Academic Block classes at John Sutter Middle School in Fowler, California. Lesa holds an M.S. in Instructional Leadership in Curriculum and Instruction. She is a Teacher Consultant for the San Joaquin Valley Writing Project.

Jared Kaiser has been teaching since 1987. He has an M.A. degree in Education with an emphasis in Math/Science from Fresno Pacific College. For the past 10 years he has taught at Bullard Talent, a fine arts magnet school in the Fresno Unified School District. Jared has been a Teacher Consultant for the San Joaquin Writing Project since 1998.

Esther Koers-Hansen has taught high school English for 5 years. She received a B.A. in English with a Women's Study minor from California State University, Fresno. She taught at an inner-city high school for 4 years and currently teaches tenth-, eleventh-, and twelfth-grade English at Hoover High School in Fresno, California. She is a Teacher Consultant for the San Joaquin Valley Writing Project.

Kathleen Markovich began teaching in 1970. She taught her entire career at Hoover High School in the Fresno Unified School District, and retired in 2006. She is a Fellow of the California Reading and Literature Project and a Teacher Consultant in the San Joaquin Valley Writing Project. Kathy has directed a variety of secondary workshops and is currently directing reading and writing in-services for teachers of grades 3–6.

Faith Nitschke is a 1993 Fellow of the San Joaquin Valley Writing Project and holds an M.A. in Composition from California State University, Fresno. She is currently a Co-Director of the San Joaquin Valley Writing Project and is a past president of the Fresno Area Council of English Teachers. She has taught English at local community colleges and California State University, Fresno, and currently works as a teacher coach at McLane High School in the Fresno Unified School District.

Michael Olenchalk, a 1998 Fellow of the San Joaquin Valley Writing Project, holds an M.A. in Education from the University of San Francisco. A life science teacher for more than 16 years, he taught at both the middle and high school levels. He served for two years as a Mentoring Director for the San Joaquin Valley Writing Project's Invitational Summer Institute. He is presently Director of the Sierra Outdoor School in Sonora, California.

Janice Peltzer is an eighth-grade teacher at Pioneer Middle School in Hanford, California, where she teaches social studies and language arts. In July 2000, she completed her fellowship with the San Joaquin Valley Writing Project and is working with the talented teachers of the Central Valley.

Joe Perez was a teacher at Chowchilla High School in Chowchilla, California for most of his career. He became a Teacher Consultant with the San Joaquin Valley Writing Project in 1980 and was a second-year fellow in 1990. He participated in numerous advanced institutes and workshops for the project. Joe has retired and is a full-time writer.

Sara Silva is a chemistry and life science teacher at Granite Hills High School in Porterville, California. She also taught seventh- and eighth-grade science at Burton Middle School in Porterville for four years. Prior to becoming a teacher, she was a scientist for over 10 years, working in a variety of laboratory settings. She was a Fellow in the San Joaquin Valley Writing Project Summer Institute in 2002.

Cynthia J. Stovall is a teacher in a special day class of students with communicative disorders, for the Fresno County Office of Education in Fresno, California. She holds a multiple-subject California credential with supplemental authorization in English, a learning handicap credential, and certification as a resource specialist. She is a member of the California Reading Association and the International Dyslexic Association. Cynthia is a Teacher Consultant for the San Joaquin Valley Writing Project.

Sarah Streib is currently an Academic Coach in the Lemoore Elementary School District, Lemoore, California. In addition to teaching in Lemoore, her other teaching experiences include teaching in both Wisconsin and Guam. She received her B.A. from the University of Wisconsin–Madison, and her M.A. in Education from the University of Wisconsin–La Crosse. Sarah is a Teacher Consultant for the San Joaquin Valley Writing Project, and a trainer for the Governor's Reading Professional Development Institutes.

Carol Surabian teaches language arts and history in Dinuba, California. She has been a Teacher Consultant for the San Joaquin Valley Writing Project since 1987. She is also a Teacher Consultant for the California History Project and the California Reading and Literature Project. An active member of the California Association of Teachers of English (CATE), she serves as president of TUCATE (Tulare County Council). She also has an M.A. in Educational Technology from Fresno Pacific University.

Gayle Taylor has been teaching in the Clovis Unified School District, Clovis, California, for over 30 years. She currently teaches English 9 and English 9 Laptop Immersion at Clovis High School. A participant in the California Professional Development Institute in 2000, she also has served as a Mentor Teacher, Team 9 Lead Teacher, English 9 Lead Teacher, and a Teacher Consultant for the San Joaquin Valley Writing Project. As a writer, she has published freelance articles in *The Fresno Bee*, poetry in *Focus* magazine, and a short story in *The San Joaquin Review*.

Gail Tompkins recently retired from teaching at California State University, Fresno, and directing the San Joaquin Valley Writing Project. She is the author of a number of literacy textbooks published by Merrill/Prentice Hall, including *Teaching Writing: Balancing Process and Product* (2007), *Literacy for the 21st Century* (2006), *Language Arts Essentials* (2006), and *Language Arts: Patterns of Practice* (2005).

Lisa Twiford has been teaching in the Delano Union Elementary School District, Delano, California, for 20 years. She is currently teaching an SEI fifth-grade class and has taught third through sixth grade, SEI classes, and GATE classes. Lisa has served as an Accelerating Literacy teacher, a mentor teacher, a Support Provider for her district's Beginning Teacher Support and Assessment program, and as a Lead Language Arts teacher. She is a Teacher Consultant for the San Joaquin Valley Writing Project.

Rebecca Wheeler is Curriculum Coordinator at McLane High School in Fresno, California, where she has taught English classes of all levels, from English Language Development and Reading to Advanced Placement. She is a Teacher Consultant with the San Joaquin Valley Writing Project, facilitates groups of teachers designing curriculum and instruction, and is actively involved with literacy efforts at her school site.

Jeffery Williams has taught for over 15 years at Clovis West High School in Clovis, California. He teaches Advanced Placement literature and remedial English and serves as a mentor and master teacher. He is a Teacher Consultant in the San Joaquin Valley Writing Project. He also dabbles in journalistic, freelance, and creative writing. Jeff has recently had his first novel, *Anne Bonney: My Pirate Story* (2006) published by iUniverse, Inc.

Karen Yelton-Curtis is a teacher at McLane High School and one of the English Department instructors for the Medical Magnet Academy. She is a Teacher Consultant and a Mentoring Director with the San Joaquin Valley Writing Project. Prior to becoming a teacher, she worked as a newspaper journalist and public relations writer for 17 years.